monsoonbooks

JAKARTA UNDERCOVER

Moammar Emka was born in the village of Jetak-Montong in East Java, Indonesia. While completing his education at the Government Institute for Islamic Studies in Jakarta, he wrote for several regional and national newspapers on social, political and religious issues.

From the mid-nineties, Moammar Emka worked for a variety of newspapers and magazines, never straying far from the world of entertainment journalism. At *Berita Yudha*, *Prospek* and *Popular*, his columns were widely read for their insights into Jakarta's popular culture and high-society life.

In addition to being a consultant and contributor at *X Men's Magazine*, a host on SCTV's 'MALEM2', a freelance writer and a photographer, Moammar Emka also runs his own business in the entertainment and public relations sector. He may be contacted at: mk_emka@yahoo.com.

JAKARTA
UNDERCOVER

MOAMMAR EMKA

monsoonbooks

Published in 2006
by Monsoon Books Pte Ltd
Blk 106 Jalan Hang Jebat #02–14, Singapore 139527
www.monsoonbooks.com.sg

First published in Indonesia in 2002
in Bahasa Indonesia by Galang Press

ISBN-13: 978-981-05-3917-7
ISBN-10: 981-05-3917-7

Cover photography by Black Studio / Collin Patrick
www.black.com.sg

Printed in Singapore
10 09 08 07 06   1 2 3 4 5 6 7 8 9

Contents

Foreword

The passing on of a tyrannical regime brings out the best and the worst of a people and their discursive consciousness. Such has been the case with the stepping aside of Indonesia's Soeharto in May 1998 and its aftermath. Moralistic groups—some genuinely puritanical and prudish, others operating more as an alternative form of thuggery—have been attacking cafés, bars, discotheques, night clubs, brothels and anything they deem immoral, including AIDS educational events. On the other hand, refreshingly celebratory events, organizations and, possibly most prominently, publications, have also cropped up in the field of sexuality.

The sexualities of ancestors, princes and princesses, prostitutes, young people, transgenders, lesbians and gay men have increasingly become the subject of writings. Unashamedly open and honest, these are a far cry from the superficial (and let it be noted, hypocritical) prudery of the Soeharto era.

The tome you have in your hand belongs to this new, post-1998 sexual spring. You will be taken by the author, Moammar Emka, on a pleasure tour of Jakarta's barely covered sexual entertainment venues and events. This is the other side of Jakarta most people either truly did not know existed or pretended they did not know about. A tad voyeuristic and more than a little titillating, it nevertheless shows the myriad possibilities in the pursuit of sexual pleasure.

This is a world where sexual orientation does not always matter, where gender can be traded in private parties, where nudity is celebrated, where bodies are appreciated with money, food or just admiring, fascinated looks.

A word of caution: reading this volume it is easy to slip into thinking that only Indonesia's capital city has such sexual facilities. Nothing is further from the truth. Other cities, even rural towns and possibly villages, have always had their sexual venues and events. It is a myth that Indonesia is a prudish society. It may be so in public articulated discourse, but in private practice, ricefields, schoolyards, religious buildings small and large, shopping malls, jogging tracks, beaches, parks, bushes and trees (yes!) are all (undercover) sexual sites, in addition to the more obvious short-time (love) hotels, beach cubicles, massage parlors, scissorless barbershops, hair salons and of course the ubiquitous brothel complexes.

The author, Moammar Emka, can boast a dyed-in-the-wool Muslim education from his childhood to his university years. As a non-religious person growing up in East Java, I have always been fascinated by the refreshingly tolerant, open and pragmatic sexual mores of the orthodox or posttraditionalist Muslims, followers of the Nahdlatul Ulama, the majority community in my province, in which Emka grew up. Generally speaking, East Javanese society is quite open towards out-of-wedlock pregnancies, cohabitation, prostitutes, transgenders, and later gay men and lesbians, especially outside family circles. This is the province that can boast an official hangout for transgenders in the capital city of Surabaya, designated by a mayoral decree in the 1980s, and if I may say so myself, the longest lasting homosexual organization in the country (1987 to the present).

Enjoy reading the Jakarta pleasure world uncovered by Emka for you. You will, I think, have a different opinion of Indonesia afterwards.

Dédé Oetomo, PhD
Founder and Trustee
GAYa NUSANTARA Foundation, Surabaya, Indonesia

Surabaya, 1 August 2005

Naked Clubbing

An underground sex party was in full swing, attended by more than 150 naked guests. Beautiful girls mingled freely with men in the basement venue, which had been designed to resemble a high-class nightclub.

Was I really to believe that such parties existed in Jakarta? Or was this just another crazy urban myth? I wondered if the impact of globalisation had finally brought our culture and social norms into such deep chaos? Had Jakarta become the Las Vegas of Asia?

My first knowledge of such underground parties—clandestine as well as subterranean—came from a famous local actor, SLA. A handsome twenty-seven year old, he was rumoured to be dating one of the sexiest actresses in Jakarta. According to SLA, while such parties may have been out of the ordinary, they were undoubtedly very real.

'The atmosphere is wild,' explained SLA. 'Really crazy and also a little scary too! We do whatever we want. We behave like kings in their harems; we're playboys for the whole night.'

As sincere as he sounded, I still needed some convincing.

These naked parties were shrouded in secrecy and were strictly members-only events. Naturally, the members were from the wealthy upper class. What surprised me more was that the parties were held uninterrupted over several days.

I had to see this for myself. I began my search by spending about a month patrolling the Pluit district of Jakarta. Based on the information I had, I guessed I would have to sniff around the luxury houses and condominiums.

I wandered around North Jakarta, where I also visited gambling dens, discotheques, karaoke bars and massage parlours. With nothing to show for my endeavours, the map I held in my mind of possible party venues was still mysteriously dark.

The breakthrough finally came when I attended a sumptuous fashion show at an international five-star hotel. It was there that I met Alex, a thirty-something man who owned a cable factory in Tangerang, twenty kilometres to the west of Jakarta. Alex was a popular guy with a wide social circle made up of friends from various ethnic backgrounds. He made a habit of attending events graced by celebrities (his wife was the owner of a luxury boutique whose customers included the rich and famous).

Alex was an articulate, easy-going guy and, after some encouragement, he opened up about his experiences of the sex entertainment scene in Jakarta. He told me he'd recently been involved in one of the underground naked parties.

Now I was getting somewhere.

'If you're on your own, the parties can be very difficult to find,' explained Alex. 'They're only for members and their guests.'

It became apparent that Alex had attended as a guest. He'd been invited by a friend, who was the owner of an upmarket discotheque in North Jakarta. And it just so happened that, based on his friend's information, another underground naked party was due to be held in several week's time. I made a date to meet up with Alex again soon.

The dusk sky above Jakarta had faded away into night's embrace. I had promised to meet Alex at a Japanese restaurant in the Kebayoran Baru district. Alex arrived with a tidily dressed, plump man.

'Let me introduce my friend,' began Alex, motioning to his friend. 'This is Hendra. It's he who invited me to go to the naked club last month.'

I shook hands with Hendra, who looked to be in his early thirties. We sat down and ordered from the menu. Over sushi and teppanyaki, we discussed matters relating to the naked club.

'The parties are usually held once a month, sometimes only once every three months,' explained Hendra. 'It depends on how many people are interested at the time. You know, everything is done secretly so only members and their guests get to know about it.'

An hour later I was whisked away in Alex's black Mercedes in the direction of Pluit. We passed Surdiman Street and entered the toll road. The conversation remained firmly fixed on the evening's entertainment.

'Jakarta is so crazy!' said an excited Alex. 'When I heard about it for the first time, I didn't believe such a thing existed here. I thought this could only happen in America or Europe. Nobody knows what we have right here on our doorstep.'

If Alex hadn't been invited by Hendra, he would never have known about it. Much less had the chance to join in.

'Instead of wasting your money travelling abroad, you're better off spending it here in Jakarta. You know, the clubs here aren't much different from the naked parties abroad,' said Hendra, with the air of a seasoned swinger.

I didn't say much as I took in the scene. I was apprehensive, but this was all leading me to what I wanted to see with my own eyes.

We entered Pluit. Alex, who was driving, was having to ask Hendra for directions. It had been a while and he clearly hadn't been paying too much attention the first time they'd made this trip.

'I've forgotten the way,' smiled Alex.

We arrived at what looked like an entertainment complex. I kept looking in all directions, a little unsettled due to my unfamiliar surroundings. As soon as we passed an old shopping mall, I realised where I was, especially when I saw a large cinema with huge film posters on display. Taking my bearings from the old mall and the cinema, I breathed a sigh of relief, happy that I recognised the landscape once more.

According to Alex, this neighbourhood belonged to the high rollers of Jakarta. The houses seemed to be part of an elite housing complex, comprising dozens of luxury detached houses and apartments. I noticed most of them had large, imposing gates.

We entered the driveway of one such house. It sure was big. There was no family nameplate or company signage on view to indicate the function of such an impressive building. Through the car windows we could see five well-built men standing in front of the main entrance. As we slowed down, two of the men quickly approached the car. The one who spoke to us was wearing jeans and a black jacket.

'Can I help you, boss?' he asked politely.

Meanwhile, the other man was leaning over, attempting to peer through the tinted windows at us. When the front passenger seat window was lowered and the man saw Hendra sitting inside, he quickly smiled and stood up, nodding to his colleague.

It seemed that they already knew Hendra very well.

'Please go to the rear parking lot,' said the first man.

From the front yard we entered the parking lot. It was huge and could probably have held more than a hundred vehicles. I noted loads of luxury cars, all neatly parked. There were BMWs, Range Rovers and Volvos—all prestige models.

Inside the parking lot we were approached by another five burly men. After double-checking who we were, one of them waved us helpfully into our parking space.

We followed Hendra up a short flight of stairs to a door that was opened by a neatly dressed man.

'Good evening, boss. Come on in,' the man greeted us.

It seemed Hendra was well known by all the staff. This made me feel safe, although I was sure I would soon be questioned and I was probably being closely watched. I reminded myself that it was impossible to get past the door unless somebody important had invited you.

Having been ushered through the entrance, we came to an inner room. Part of the room was set up like a restaurant. There was even a small bar. Waiters were busy serving guests.

'This is the starting place. It's a bit like the lobby of a hotel,' whispered Hendra before turning to face one of the waiters. Respectfully, he asked, 'Would you tell your boss that Hendra has arrived?'

The waiter nodded and briskly walked off to find his superior.

We chose a table near the bar. I noticed the room seemed to be like the inside of a Japanese or Chinese restaurant. None of the furnishings were begging for attention. The most decadent items on display were some typical Chinese paper decorations resembling curtains and some pictures hanging on the wall.

A short while later we were approached by a well-groomed man dressed in suit and tie.

'Mr Hendra, how are you doing?' asked the man warmly. 'This is your guest from before, is it not?' he continued, turning now to Alex.

The man's name, I had gathered, was Robby, and he was the owner of the club. He was thirty-four years old. Hendra introduced me as his close friend (while not actually elaborating as to how exactly he knew me). As Hendra's guest I was accepted warmly, despite the fact that I wasn't as well dressed as they were and I was clearly an outsider.

I listened intently to them talking about business. Mutual trust appeared to play a very important role both in their personal relationship and in their work dealings. I could sense that these were the sort of people who frequently shook hands on a deal without worrying about the need for a written contract.

It was now eight thirty. Robby had already ordered several rounds of drinks.

'How is your place doing? Are you getting more guests?' asked Hendra.

'Well, the parties last for the same time as before and the membership is increasing. As you can see now, it's crowded,' answered Robby, while gulping down his drink. 'By the way, do you want to join in or are you just dropping by?'

'I've been here before so I think it would be impossible for me to just drop by now!' laughed Hendra. 'The 'collection' is getting more varied, isn't it?'

'Of course. If I don't add to the collection, the members will get bored, you know,' answered Robby, also laughing.

We left our seats and were led down a flight of stairs which was lit by neon strip lights. We now appeared to be in the basement but the interior was completely different to what we'd seen upstairs. Four receptionists welcomed us with friendly smiles. There was a big door to the side of the reception desk, which seemed to be securely locked. I sat on a sofa while waiting patiently for Alex and Hendra, who were still talking to Robby. I looked around me. The walls were painted an earthy colour. Dimly lit lamps in each corner of the room cast a soft glow of light. To the other side of the reception desk was a second door.

Robby excused himself and began to take his leave.

'Have a good time,' he said.

Two receptionists approached us and invited us to go through the second door.

'Sorry, but could you take off all of your clothes, please? You don't need to bring your watch, mobile phone or wallet with you. Please leave all of your things in the boxes provided. We'll lock the boxes safely,' explained one of the receptionists.

After being ushered through the door, we saw a row of boxes as promised. We removed our clothes until we were standing completely naked. A black curtain now confronted us. It seemed that behind the black curtain I would find all my answers.

I pulled back the curtain and even though I knew what was coming, the sight that greeted me still managed to startle me. My God! What I saw took my breath away. It was just like any other nightclub scene— thunderous music, hundreds of people dancing and chatting—only this time all of the guests were stark naked. Nobody was wearing anything!

We entered the party and I split from the others. Hendra and Alex were soon mingling with other guests, clearly having a good time. I looked around the room. The interior was decorated in a brown, clay-flavoured hue. I felt like I was in a late Mediterranean sunset. The lamps were dim, the room bordering on dark, although the vision I was getting of the naked club could not have been clearer and more transparent!

I took stock of the people that were inside. The male guests were representative of many ethnic backgrounds. I noticed among them some Indonesian television celebrities. The women were plentiful; there were Arabs, Chinese, Indians and Caucasians, but the majority were *pribumi* or indigenous Indonesian. I couldn't believe that there were so many beautiful, sexy, voluptuous women before my very eyes. Their behaviour was wild and they were certainly enticing.

Inside a large island bar in the centre of the room, four naked women poured all manner of alcoholic drinks for the guests. Naked bartenders! In each corner of the room were tables overflowing with fine food, beautifully presented and there for the taking.

I noticed some side rooms but could not see inside, their entrances were covered by curtains.

On a small stage close to the bar, several women were undulating and gyrating to the music as they performed a striptease. I felt I was now in dreamland.

In every direction all I could see were beautiful naked women; it was enough to make a man both nervous and very excitable! I saw couples and groups coming and going from the curtained-off rooms. Two women with one man or vice versa. Everything and anything seemed to be happening and it was mind-bending to take it all in.

Was this for real? My world had just been turned upside down. Until now, I could only see such exciting scenes in blue movies, and here I was seeing it all live, in the flesh and in 3D! I murmured to myself, marvelling at the bizarreness of it all.

I was so absorbed that I didn't know how long I'd been in this under-ground room full of volcanic lust. I had lost all concept of time. Staying in this room was like never experiencing daylight. It was beginning to feel like a dream, which no morning light could awake me from.

It was now almost five o'clock in the morning. I rejoined Hendra and Alex, and we left the naked party, exhausted and weary. My friends appeared to have been busy, judging by their smiles and relaxed manner.

'Wow, Rani's massage was great. Not to mention her extra service,' said Alex, smiling.

After getting dressed and tipping the two receptionists, we climbed the neon-lit stairs back up to the lobby. Without any further delay, we headed to the car in the parking lot and drove off.

On the way back we talked about what we'd experienced in the club. As we passed through the quiet, early morning streets of Jakarta, Hendra and Alex reflected once again on the difficulty of gaining access to the club.

In order to become a member, you had to pay an upfront fee of Rp50 million (US$5000) for a six-month period, after which you had to pay a further Rp3 million (US$300) to attend each party.

'If you're strong, you can enjoy the party for two days and two nights,' commented Hendra.

I tried to imagine lasting that long. From what I'd just experienced, that was some going!

Hendra also explained that the beautiful 'ladies in waiting' at the party were specially selected; 'obtained' from a number of high-class procurers in Jakarta. On average, each girl was paid between Rp5 to 10 million (US$500 to 1000) for each two-day-long party.

We finally came to a stop at a four-star hotel in the Block M district. We wanted to take a room each for a much-needed rest. Once inside my hotel room, I could still picture what I had seen in the naked club: dozens of naked, sexy girls with their tempting, erotic dancing.

Triple-service VIP Sauna Special

Imagine a sauna service that offers men such flirtatious treatments as a comforting body massage, skin lightening treatment using herbal cosmetics, perhaps even a pedicure ... all of this performed by a beautiful girl. Add a second girl and you have a Double-service Sauna Special, add a third and you have the ultimate in uplifting VIP sauna treatments: the Triple-service VIP Sauna Special.

It's not as exotic as it sounds. For many people, a steam bath or sauna, coupled with the invigorating services of beautiful girls, had become a favourite pastime.

The steam bath, or sauna, is not a new thing to Jakarta. Saunas can be found in nearly every part of the city. From high-class fitness centres and luxury office buildings to seedy massage parlours, the sauna has become a way of life.

There are saunas in luxury hotels in Thamrin Street and Surdiman Street, while others are mushrooming in the Kebayoran Baru and Tebet districts, both areas synonymous with beauty parlours in Jakarta. The average sauna room is comfortable and exclusive. Customers are normally male executives, but there are also some saunas catering to well-heeled women.

As expected, most saunas are single sex—separate rooms for men and women. But an increasing number are deviating from this practice.

One such establishment is located at the infamous CP.

When Jakarta was awash with massage parlours, steam baths, pubs, and nightclubs in the 1980s, CP was a focus for the glamour and glitter of high-class night entertainment. This was primarily due to its location: next to a four-star hotel in Ancol. CP is not only famous for its private saunas but also for its casino.

With so many competing entertainment venues offering similar services such as restaurants, nightclubs, fitness facilities, saunas and so on, what makes CP so special that it still attracts men in droves?

Well, what else, if not because of its special sauna services? Thanks to its reputation over the years, it remains popular, even though its saunas are not as luxurious as those found in the newer fitness centres in five-star hotels. Despite the rather decrepit state of its interior with its rather dim and dreary lighting, CP has it's own special allure, thanks to a glorious history.

I decided to pay CP a visit. In its main anteroom, sitting on benches and sofas, and chatting together, were a large number of middle-aged men and some younger guys. It seemed a big crowd for seven o'clock on a Wednesday evening. The place is busiest just after lunch time, not to mention the nights before public holidays and on most Friday or Saturday evenings.

'There are lots of guests who, having dined at the café, and maybe won on the gambling tables, come here to relax, trying to ease their muscles,' said Bram, a friend who accompanied me to CP. Bram, a twenty-nine-year-old manager at a café in Senayan, was a useful guide as he was a member at CP and consequently had access to more than just the normal service, which is what I would have received.

'Normal service?' I queried.

'Yes, paying the entrance ticket alone will just get you standard massages,' replied Bram.

I had to admit that I still didn't understand exactly what he meant. As I understood it, fitness centre guests could use the facilities by paying a standard entrance fee and for this they would get a one-hour massage, a sauna, and a bath with warm or cold water, after which they could continue to use the other fitness facilities.

What I was now discovering was that by paying Rp250,000 (US$25) per hour for VIP rooms, a guest could get sauna facilities but he would also be accompanied by a hostess of his choice.

'If you want the special service, you can order directly through the 'mammy" added Bram. The term mammy refers to the mamasan, who coordinates the girls and who is herself often a masseuse.

Bram, being a paid-up member of CP, was close to Mammy Neny. With a beautiful face, stylishly made up, Mammy Neny looked friendly and approachable, even though from the way she smoked incessantly she seemed to be worried and nervous.

As a coordinator, Mammy Neny certainly had a lot of experience to draw upon. Bram said that she used to be a hostess, but then became the girlfriend of a boss who was one of her clients. Everything that Neny needed was fulfilled by her boyfriend, the boss. However, about a year into their relationship, her boyfriend left when he became bored with her. Neny could do nothing, except return to her old profession.

One year later, because of her good relationship with the bosses at CP, Neny was promoted to mammy. As a mammy, Neny also paid special attention to a number of important guests, who were either her bosses or long-standing customers of CP.

'There are also members of local authorities who, if they happen to be staying in the hotel next to us, drop by here,' Neny explained.

Bram suggested I order a Triple-service VIP Sauna Special. I agreed and arranged three masseuses: one for Bram and two for me. The three women that Mammy Neny chose were what the house termed 'prima donnas', although it's quite possible that this is what they're all called!

In other health parlours the guests usually chose their masseuse from a selection of photos, whereas at CP you are free to meet the hostesses in person. Indeed, Mammy Neny's selection wasn't bad at all.

Lisa, who became Bram's hostess, had white skin and a fit body, while Evi and Rita had well-defined facial features and sharp noses.

Bram and I entered a VIP room, apparently named after an exotic flower. The room was about four metres by five metres, with a minibar. On one side was a smaller room, which was partitioned with a curtain. I was surprised because the room was similar to a hotel room. There was one big bed with a clean white bed sheet. Large mirrors were attached to two of the walls. There was also a television set and a hi-fi system. Opening the curtain to the smaller room revealed an all-in-one bathtub and sauna. 'Welcome to B Room' was written on a small card on the table, beside two glasses of whiskey and coke and a glass of vodka and orange.

'Have a bath, a drink, or a massage first?' asked Evi hospitably, startling me.

I didn't know what to say. Evi suddenly took off her clothes, leaving only her bra covering her breasts, and her panties. Oh my God!

'Hey, why are you so dazed? Nervous or excited?' joked Rita while guiding me towards a seat and beckoning me to pull off my clothes.

Evi and Rita adeptly helped me remove my clothes piece by piece and then exchanged them for a bathrobe.

'You don't want to get your clothes wet, do you?' asked Evi, smiling.

Then, without saying any more, Evi ushered me towards the bathtub. I could do nothing but comply with her like a bashful kid.

I was treated like a prince. Finding myself bathed by beautiful, engaging girls was certainly a first. As much as I was enjoying myself, I felt clumsy because I was wearing nothing, and they were almost naked themselves.

I felt even more awkward as they aroused and tempted me, shamelessly playing with me. They rubbed me with soap, cleaned and kneaded my fingers, and trimmed my nails. They entered the bathtub by turns or together, always moving closer to me. Their sensual movement and stroking frequently excited me.

I didn't know how the other male guests could stand the seduction of such beautiful devils.

A Celine Dion song was filling the warm room. As I bathed in the soft light I wondered whether I could contain myself any longer. But before I could answer my own question, Evi asked me to get up. She covered her body with a towel in order to help our bodies absorb the sauna's vapours. As we chatted we could feel our bodies warming gradually, our drinks going down nicely. How relaxing, I thought to myself.

The stories were classic, if clichéd. I couldn't remember how many times I'd heard of similar stories from women working in places such as these. Having been frustrated and unjustly treated by men, both Evi and Rita admitted they'd become victims.

I listened attentively to their stories.

Evi had been betrayed by her boyfriend, whom she met when they were university students in Medan, Sumatra. Rita's experience was worse than Evi's as she came to realise her boyfriend, whom she'd trusted implicitly, only used her for her body.

'We're stupid because we're willing to be used by men. We've been ruined. We lost everything and got nothing in return. It's still better to get something, because, you know, we all like to get handfuls of gold and diamonds ...' said Evi, smiling grimly.

A few minutes later I was back on the bed for my massage. Time passed rapidly as Rita and Evi skillfully continued their service. When I looked at my watch, it was already eight o'clock (I had arrived just after seven). It seemed that the one-hour slot was too short to get the full service.

I was still thinking about this when both of them offered to lengthen the session. Wearing a bathrobe and underwear only, Rita climbed slowly onto my back, while Evi massaged my face seductively. Can you imagine it? This wasn't the massage of a lady-in-waiting. It was a rub full of temptation, which could overpower the flavour of even the world's most full-bodied wine!

My instincts were right. Evi soon offered a little more than we had seen up till then.

'What about Rita?' I stalled.

'Why? Not interested in me?' whined Evi. 'OK, how about if we all join in? You've never tried a threesome have you? Come on ... let's try it now ...'

For a while I was left speechless. But it transpired that this offer of a special massage was simply a sex transaction. This was more than I had been expecting. This extra, full service could be enjoyed not only on the bed but also in the steam bath, depending on the guests' wishes. The most important thing though seemed to be that an agreement be reached between both parties about the amount of tips.

'What do you actually want?' asked Evi, sulkily. 'If you don't want to do it on the bed, we can go to the steam bath. You know, lots people are very fond of doing it in the steam bath.'

Sorry, I thought to myself, but I just can't go through with this. I feigned disinterest and decided to end the service. I told the girls that I thought that one hour was more than enough, although I was sure that most male guests experienced the special full service.

I completely understood if the girls were upset because basically they'd lost the chance to earn the extra money. In fact, for one full service they were supposed to get between Rp200,000 and Rp300,000 (US$20 to US$30). I did sympathise when their faces expressed disappointment but I reassured myself that I had given them a decent amount of money in tips.

The massage offered by CP was patently intended to lead into a short-time sex service and it seemed that this tendency had spread to many places, although not all places were like this of course.

I asked Bram about this.

'Now, let's just think about it realistically,' Bram explained. 'What will happen if a man and a masseuse are in close proximity in a closed room? Even if they haven't had sex, it's still possible it will head in that direction. The man may be looking for physical satisfaction, while the woman needs money. You know, the opportunity is very big for them to satisfy each other's needs. If it's not convenient to do the transaction then and there, they can always do it in other more convenient places like a hotel.'

'But the Triple-service VIP Sauna Special?' I asked, pretending to be naive.

'What's wrong with a threesome? They block out their feelings. They don't care whether it's double, triple or even quadruple. They treat it the same. Actually, if it's triple or more, it's better for them because they work less; the job is easier, the effort is divided ...' Bram replied facetiously.

The special service at CP is no longer unusual; such services can now be found in other places such as massage parlors, discotheques and nightclubs. However, as I said before, the types of the package offered are different wherever you go. It's like a chef who must try to find unusual flavours and spices in order to make the food more interesting. Similarly, the services offered by these places need the same variety.

Squeals on Wheels

Fast cars. Fast women. It was only a matter of time before 'sex-for-sale in SUVs' (sports utility vehicles) became the latest item on the menu in Jakarta. What is it with guys and cars?

Many people say that sex is not just sex, it's also a game. Sex, it seems, cannot be separated from adventure, so it's not surprising when a variety of games are purposely offered to satisfy adventurous men. When it comes to providing striptease dancing, erotic bathing and other interesting enticements, Jakarta never seems to run out of sexual gasoline.

In the name of improved business, entertainment establishments are finding new and exciting ways to attract customers, and there aren't many more thrilling activities for a willing male, than having sex in a moving car. Added to which, it also presents a practical challenge!

I discovered this phenomenon through talking with a friend. Andreas, a thirty-one-year-old stock broker, was blessed with a wide group of friends, from children of officials to those from the burgeoning café community; the sort who seemed to be very fond of hanging out at night.

As a sociable and personable young professional, Andreas belonged to the group of men who were never satisfied with the standard fare that was currently on offer in Jakarta. He frequently imagined being able to enjoy an alternative type of love service.

'What's important about sex is the adventure,' stressed Andreas.

He had already imagined making love to a woman in a car. He'd never tried to do it, but he certainly didn't consider it to be unusual or unobtainable.

'Is there a sex service offered in a moving car, complete with a driver, and facilities such as a bed, food and drinks?' asked Andreas one day.

There are lots of men who really want to pour out their sexual lust in alternative ways, beyond what others would consider normal. Sex in beds, swimming pools and even public places no longer posed a challenge for Andreas. Sex in a chauffeur-driven SUV, however, seemed to him like the ultimate original fantasy. As it turned out, Andreas was not alone. It appeared there was no shortage of men in Jakarta wanting to attain paradise on earth with a beautiful woman in the back of a four-wheel drive as it navigated the streets of the capital—the world's fourth largest city.

At first, I presumed that sex in moving cars took place somewhere in North Jakarta, maybe at Ancol, where the 'shaking car' phenomenon has been a common sight in secluded carparks for years. But instead, I found myself heading into the city at the invitation of Andreas and his friend Gunawan. Thirty-three-year-old Gunawan was big shot in a hip advertising agency that dealt with international clients, and his expensive branded clothes identified him as belonging to Jakarta's elite.

Andreas chatted to Gunawan, while nodding in my direction. 'This time he'll be the male rabbit. You can't get too excited any more Gunawan,' teased Andreas.

I just smiled at them. Andreas was referring to Gunawan's numerous previous visits. It was Gunawan who had shown Andreas what this sex in cars was all about.

From GM plaza we doubled back, then entered a side alley wide enough to accommodate two cars. We crawled on a little further, aiming for a building shrouded in red and green light, which shone bright in the fading light of the day that was slowly turning into night.

On closer inspection we could see that the red and green light was from a neon sign depicting a moon and a bird, and a logo: 'ML'.

In the carpark, to the side of the building, were loads of luxury cars, including BMWs and Mercs. A parking attendant helped us find a spot to park Andreas' SUV.

'Well, this is the place. Are you ready for an adventure?' asked Gunawan, smiling cheekily.

It was seven o'clock when we entered the building. We were welcomed by a female attendant who was wearing a black jacket over a white shirt, and a miniskirt. With a friendly smile, she invited us in. My immediate reaction was that I didn't like the surroundings. It seemed like an office, but it wasn't. If it was a café, it didn't look like one. But it certainly was full of people.

I could hear music. The rhythm was soft and slow, seductive even. The lamps shone quite brightly. At first glance, ML appeared to be a combination of a café and a discotheque. We looked around the room. We could see dapper men, and sexy ladies wearing tight T-shirts and miniskirts.

We were invited to take a seat. A waitress came over to us and offered some menus. We ordered a glass of white wine and two glasses of Black Russian. A few minutes later, the waitress, who must have been about thirty-five, returned with our drinks.

'Please enjoy yourself. Would you like to order something else?' she asked politely. We all shook our heads.

The waitress then introduced herself as Irma. Although not particularly beautiful, she was nicely made up.

'Would the three of you like some company?' asked Irma as she leaned over to serve our drinks. Her question didn't seem to faze Gunawan, who immediately got down to business.

31

'Well, could you provide us with the 'Indo-menus'?' he asked.

'OK, sure. Come on, follow me,' she smiled.

We followed Irma into a backroom, one section of which was partitioned off by glass walls. Inside this oversize fishbowl sat a posse of young women who were happily chatting away to each other. Some had more slanted eyes, others had more defined, sharp noses, while the rest had classic Indonesian facial features. It looked exactly like an aquarium of ornamental fish.

'Take your pick,' gestured Irma towards the fishbowl. 'The one with the curly hair and sharp nose is Reni, she's twenty-two. Of course that's not actually her real name, in the world of 'evening entertainment' nobody uses their real name. Reni's originally from Sukabumi. The fair-skinned one with the hourglass figure is Babby … she's twenty-five. The curvaceous one is Fara, she just turned twenty. Her service comes with a guarantee of satisfaction!'

In this way, Irma continued to introduce all of her 'pupils' while expounding their various merits. When done, she led us into another, more comfortable room. Without even ordering, we were once again served drinks. Irma soon returned with two beautiful looking girls, who we hadn't seen in the fishbowl. They were introduced to us as Dina and Rosa. From their looks, style and physique they both gave the impression they were Caucasian; they were probably mixed.

Dina and Rosa were polite and friendly as they made small talk about jobs and colleagues. The 170-centimetre-tall Rosa admitted to her Western roots.

'I'm from Central Java. My mother is from Semarang, but my father is from Holland,' she said gently.

Rosa must have sensed what we were thinking.

'Don't be surprised. You might recognize my face from TV. I've been in some productions that you may have seen on the television.'

Prior to working here, Rosa told us that she used to work as a freelance escort. She had even gone to college, but quit due to a lack of money. Perhaps it was a little trite to say this, but it's true that Jakarta is a very money-orientated environment, and without it, progress can be very tough. Rosa found herself taking the quickest route to making money, which was 'selling love' to executives and company bosses.

'I haven't been working here for very long ... maybe only five months, but I need the money and it's fun too,' reaffirmed Rosa.

Meanwhile, Dina, whom I thought very beautiful with her bright skin and shoulder-length hair, was from Bandung and of Arab descent. That explained her elegant sharp nose!

'Actually, I used to work for an insurance company, but I'm taking a break to do this. My needs this month have increased dramatically,' she said.

We gathered that Dina and Rosa were prima donnas at ML, and that they both preferred to stay out of the limelight. The fishbowl was not for them. As they were fortunate enough to have a reasonably regular clientele, they didn't feel the need to advertise their wares so bluntly.

'I feel uncomfortable if I'm placed in the fishbowl,' Dina said seriously.

I looked at Dina again. Her lips and hair resembled Pamela Anderson's, although she had a sharper nose. She had worked as a photographic model before joining the insurance company, but neither job offered her the financial rewards of being a 'squeals-on-wheels' girl. With just one job, she could pocket Rp2 to 3 million (US$200 to 300).

It was already seven forty-five when we decided to begin our tour. We called Irma, who was busy welcoming more guests. As soon as we got up from our seats, Irma asked Dina and Rosa to get ready.

Irma guided us to a large garage containing Pajeros, Blazers, Range Rovers, Land Cruisers and other luxury local and imported SUVs.

'What kind of car do you want to use?' asked Irma. She pointed at a dark blue Range Rover. 'This one was once specially requested by … well, by someone who has been summoned frequently by the Attorney General.'

Andreas settled on a locally made Pajero. I noticed a smiling Gunawan, together with Rosa, also choosing the same.

Irma then led us to a room guarded by two beautiful women. It was in this room that Andreas paid for the service.

'Do you want to pay cash?' they asked.

Andreas preferred to pay by credit card rather than cash. It cost Rp5 million (US$500) for the Pajero whereas the Range Rover was Rp7 million (US$700). The price included the 'date' and was for one tour, which would last between three and four hours.

I walked around the room while Andreas was sorting out the payment. These vehicles all looked completely normal from the outside. I moved towards the silver Pajero and saw that it had tinted windows. The driver, a well-dressed middle-aged man, opened the back door as he spoke to me.

'Using this one, boss?' he asked.

He must have presumed I was his guest for the evening. I looked inside the car. It seemed that the interior had been specially designed for this unusual tour. Inside there was a kind of sofa without it's back, and a mini dining table on which some food and drinks were placed. I could see that the space was also fitted with a telephone and sophisticated audio-visual equipment. It seemed that everything was in place for an evening's mobile entertainment.

For more privacy, the driver and passenger sections of the car were separated by a glass partition protected by a curtain on the passenger side to prevent the front passengers from seeing into the back. And, because of the tinted windows, people outside the car could only see the vague outlines of the passengers within, while those inside could see out as normal.

'OK, let me ride with the driver in the front,' I said to Andreas and Gunawan. 'Enjoy yourselves!'

Actually, they really wanted me to join them in their adventure but I politely refused. It occurred to me that Rp5 million (US$500) seemed to be nothing to them.

'Come on, join us. I'll treat you,' coaxed Andreas.

'No, thanks. Next time, perhaps.'

We set off in the Pajero, and were soon heading across Jakarta. Soft music was playing to a slow rhythm in the car. It was cooling down as evening set in.

As I smoked a cigarette, I wondered what Andreas and Gunawan were doing inside the back room of their cars.

I didn't know where the idea for sex in a moving car had come from. Maybe it had been adapted from drive-in dating. Or maybe it was inspired by Hollywood movies featuring scenes of orgies in limousines. Was it a safe way of having sex under the apparent gaze of so many people, but who actually couldn't see you. Or do guys just love cars?

Whatever its origins, according to Andreas, the business of sex-for-sale in SUVs was growing among shady entrepreneurs.

'What we always seek is excitement in our fantasies. Sex in a hotel is something very common, very normal, but how about in a moving car on the streets, just yards away from the public? That's why sex in moving cars is so popular,' said Andreas.

I was sure that he was right, but also surprised at the nerve of running such a business, which was clearly illegal.

As if reading my thoughts, Andreas added, 'Nowadays it seems every business in Jakarta breaks the rules to a certain extent. Everything runs smoothly though, doesn't it? Even this business and it's supposed to be a secret!'

It was clearly a growing business. In the last two years the number of clients was on the up, even though they mainly came from the monied classes. According to Mr Tri, the driver of our Pajero, those interested in the service were mostly rich bosses, both Chinese Indonesian and *pribumi*.

After touring around Jakarta for almost two hours, our car slowly joined the streets headed towards the city. From Tomang we continued to Silang Monas, then slowly passed Thamrin. After turning around Tugu Selamat Datang at the roundabout in front of the Indonesia Hotel, we drove down Surdiman Street, turning to Semanggi Bridge, and then went directly to Block M.

At about eleven-thirty, the car entered the Harmoni district. This meant that we'd spent almost three hours crisscrossing Jakarta. As we arrived back at ML, I saw the car that Gunawan and Rosa had used, already parked. It seemed that they had returned before us.

'Hmm, wasn't it exciting?' teased Gunawan when he met Andreas in the bar.

'Not bad,' agreed Andreas, smiling.

Rosa looked happy but maybe she was just being professional. It seemed at odds with the reality of the situation; a traceless transaction with no real emotions involved. Maybe the location and X-factor (be it the girl or the service) were different every time for the client, but for Rosa and her colleagues, this was just another day at the office.

'But that's the main enjoyment,' said Andreas when we began to debate again.

Before finishing our talk, they had even invited me to see another similar place. The squeals-on-wheels service was not only offered by ML but also by another company, known as KU, which operated as an event organiser for seminars and tourist activities. KU wasn't far from M Hotel, which was located in the city area. In its operation, however, KU frequently used the services of touts, who put them in touch with groups of executives who would become regular guests.

For men like Gunawan and Andreas, the X-factor was the most

important thing when they tried to seek new adventures.

And it will continue to be so.

Arabian Nights Bachelor Party

An import from the West, the Bachelor Party is becoming de rigueur among Jakarta's elite.

It is now compulsory for a soon-to-be-wed young man from the upper classes to hold a bachelor party for his close friends in a discotheque, club, café or private room. The high-flyers and celebrities in Jakarta, and those accustomed to the party scene, now think nothing of attending such events. As if to remind the single man of what he is giving up when married, the whiff of sex is ever present.

I'd been attending these parties for several years and but never fully understood them. As in the West, they were often themed, so one could enjoy a Las Vegas party, a Hawaiian party or maybe an Arabian nights party.

One party, which I recall vividly, was memorable for many reasons other than its theme! I will never forget it. It lasted all night, was held in several locations and certainly had enough action to keep me interested. The story began when I met Roy, a friend of mine, one Friday evening at the Hard Rock Café.

Roy, who was about thirty-one years old then, was the owner of a container shipping company in Jakarta, and he was also involved in running a ceramics business.

I don't remember how many times previously I'd met up with Roy.

We often met up at the weekends to visit entertainment venues in Jakarta. But this time things were different. Roy told me that he was about to get married. Naturally, before giving up his single status, his friends and business colleagues wanted to throw him a bachelor party.

'Tomorrow, you'll have to come. I'll wait for you at nine o'clock, OK?' he said, as we were sitting at a table drinking Long Island Teas.

I was curious to know what kind of party this was going to be, so I accepted Roy's invitation. I knew that Roy and his friends really liked to party, so it was fairly safe to assume the evening would involve gorgeous girls.

It was eight fifteen the following evening when I set off to meet Roy. I was a little early, so hung out at our arranged meeting place, the ZB café in Block M. Coincidentally, some other friends of mine were already there, enjoying a drink after work. I wondered if they were here because ZB café also offered a striptease dance package for its guests.

In the carpark I met a friend of Roy's, called Budi. Besides being Roy's friend, Budi, who was twenty-eight, was also his partner in the ceramics business.

Budi and I walked along together.

'Roy's been waiting for us on the second floor,' he said.

'I know, he called me earlier and asked me to go directly to the VIP room,' I replied.

We found the VIP room in which they were playing jazz. Inside were a pair of long sofas and one table, and a wide selection of alcohol.

Roy welcomed us with his trademark laughter. There were seven more of Roy's friends with him, all sitting on the sofas. I recognized four of them from previous nights out with Roy.

'These are my business colleagues. You know how it is, all of us trying to make a living, trying to keep our heads above water,' he said, giggling.

'So, are we ready for the show?' Roy asked, as he pressed a bell to summon a waitress.

The room was dimly lit. The television that had been showing music videos was suddenly turned off and I noticed the music in the room was now louder than before. We all perked up when five beautiful women walked in. They began dancing and before we knew it, were seductively removing their clothes.

This unexpected live show was very enjoyable indeed but it was about to get more interesting. Roy's friends clearly had something else planned.

'Let's give him a surprise tonight,' whispered Budi.

I watched in amazement as the others tied Roy to a chair. He could do nothing as five naked women danced around him. He was getting flustered as they directed their sensual moves in his direction. His friends were enjoying this hugely, laughing and joking as they knocked back their drinks. Roy was closing his eyes, trying to stay calm, but sure enough his friends continued to tease him.

'Come on, where's your virility? Show it now!' they shouted.

By now Roy was completely naked. The girls kept on writhing and undulating their sexy bodies around Roy. Understandably, Roy could no longer restrain his sexual lust. How could he hold it back? The striptease dancers repeatedly and deliberately rubbed and kneaded every part of his body ... and I mean every part! What made it worse was that Roy couldn't move his body at all because he was still tied to the chair.

'For mercy's sake!' he shouted repeatedly.

This went on for an interminably long time. Eventually the ordeal was over and his friends released him, laughing uproariously as they did so. Roy's face was bright red and he was sweating profusely.

By now the striptease dancers had already put their clothes back on and I assumed that this was to be the end of all the fun. I was wrong.

Roy's friends took out a worn T-shirt and a crumpled pair of shorts.

'Hey, what are you up to now?' Roy protested, as we forced him to put on these tatty clothes.

We led him down the corridor and into the parking lot. Roy couldn't hide his embarrassment as we passed some escort girls in the lobby. He clearly had no idea what was in store for him.

We took Roy, in his tatty clothes and bare feet, to a four-star hotel in the Matraman district. It was ten thirty when we arrived, but Budi and his friends had already reserved a suite. The planning involved was evident when we were greeted by two guards, who nodded knowingly when Budi asked them if everything was ready.

On entering the hotel suite, we were welcomed by two women wearing veils. Apart from their veils, they wore only Aladdin-style pantaloons and elaborate bras, revealing their bare stomachs.

Also present were around ten other guests who had arrived separately. These men were friends and business associates of Roy.

'This must have been your doing, my friend,' said Roy as he playfully punched Budi. They laughed together as they surveyed the scene. A selection of food and drink was arranged on several small tables positioned around the room. A large, colourful rug covering the floor completed the Middle Eastern theme.

Five waitresses wearing thin veils attended to the guests. Underneath their light veils we could see bright red lipstick and very colourful eye shadow. Their breasts were prominent, thanks to their skimpy bras. Their navels drew our attention as well. Such attractive bare flesh was a sight for sore eyes.

Two mesmerising desert songs, 'Habibie' and 'Aisyah', played softly in the background. The atmosphere was exhilarating.

Roy invited everyone to join in a toast.

'You know, not long after this party I will be a married man,' he said, while raising a glass of red wine. 'This is my last night as a single man. I think you'll agree this calls for a celebration!'

The volume of the Arabian music increased. From a side room, ten girls appeared. They were only scantily clothed, with very thin and revealing linens loosely covering their bodies.

The dancing began. We watched them shimmy backwards and forwards as they tempted us with their taught yet rolling bellies. Some of the guests moved in and began dancing with the girls. They were welcomed openly and the girls didn't seem to mind as the men casually placed their hands close to the womens' breasts. This only added to the charged atmosphere and as various alcoholic drinks began to take effect the men became a little bolder and with it the dancing more adventurous.

The girls moved from one man to another, offering drinks as they did so. The guests were becoming more daring as they imbibed more alcohol. They hugged and passionately embraced the waitresses and dancers, who seemed to be prepared for everything. Some of the men were determined to trace the dancers' bodies, especially the sensitive parts of their body, with their noses! This was becoming a free for all.

In each corner of the room, a couple could be seen being intimate with each other. Some were kissing and groping each other madly. Others were just chatting. Roy meanwhile, was absorbed with a waitress.

The fumes from the alcohol mixed with the heavy, sweet clouds of clove cigarette smoke. The voices of drunken men and flirtatious girls filled the room, an unexpected and heady cocktail indeed.

A couple of hours later I awoke to survey the scene. Roy seemed to have slept soundly on a sofa. Next to him, sprawled in an ungainly manner was a girl whose clothes were in a complete mess. Budi was relaxing, sitting down, and sipping a glass of warm tea. A beautiful girl accompanied him. She was still wearing the same clothes as the night before. Her make-up and veils had gone and her creamy skin appeared to be even more beautiful and fresher in its natural condition—the natural beauty of an indigenous Indonesian girl.

The room was emptier than on the previous night. Some of the guests must have gone home already.

'Good morning. Want to join us?' Budi offered. I agreed and went over to chat with them.

They told me that an events company based in Jakarta had put together the Arabian Nights party. The girls behind the veils weren't actually of Arabic descent, rather they were local girls dressed up to look as Arabian as possible.

Budi's lady friend was introduced to me as Remy from Tasikmalaya in West Java. She worked full-time through an agency as a dancer and a social escort. Budi told me that the previous night's package had cost Rp20 million (US$2000).

'It depends on the type of package,' he said. 'The more expensive the package is, the crazier the party will be.'

I could well believe it.

Chicken Nights

Living the expatriate dream, thousands of miles from their home countries, in exotic surroundings with beautiful girls aplenty, some Western men in Jakarta have redefined the classic dinner party.

A lot of Westerners in Jakarta have local women as girlfriends, lovers or 'secret spouses'. Of the myriad call girls working in Jakarta, many specialise in making themselves available to Western men. Their services range from single sessions to longer-term casual relationships without the commitment of marriage.

So it was perhaps not surprising then to find call girls wandering around the nightclubs and entertainment venues frequented by Caucasian men. The JC café in Senayan, the TM discotheque in Tanah Abang, or the BT café in a five-star hotel in Surdiman, for example, were always replete with women of the night looking to catch their prey.

I'd been observing this scene for some time but one experience stands out as being more than a little unusual. A friend of mine, Johan, or Jo, had invited me to a party in a luxury house. Jo was thirty years old and a marketing director for an advertising company that had many foreign clients.

This was the third time that Jo had invited me to such a party. I'd been to one in the late nineties where all the guests were expected to remove an item of clothing as soon as they walked in. I recall it being a riotous affair, with many naked men and women dancing and drinking well into the early hours.

Several years later I had another chance to meet up with Jo. I hadn't been in contact with him for six months, mainly because he had been working in Singapore.

We met in our favourite place, the BQ café at Plaza Senayan. This was where we often enjoyed coffees, talking about our late-night adventures in Jakarta.

As a marketing director, Jo is not someone who likes sitting behind a desk all day long. With an enviable position in a reputable company, Jo belongs to a breed of young executives who have no material worries. And that is without mentioning his privileged background, coming as he does, from a wealthy family.

So it's fair to say that Jo enjoys a very cosmopolitan life. He's well known around the clubbing scene in Jakarta, where he's regularly seen at his favourite venues, such as Zanzibar and Prego in Iskandarsyah Street or the Hard Rock Café in Thamrin Street. His hobnobbing with socialites earned him lots of inside information about the underground sex scene in Jakarta.

It was seven thirty as we drank our third beer together. The BQ café was very crowded; indeed all the tables were full.

'Time to go!' announced Jo.

I thought it was a pity to be leaving so soon. The café was full of cute girls and I was enjoying the view. Jo told me that the party was supposed to start at seven but that he didn't want to be too early, so now was a good time to get going.

'The best part isn't the dinner. It's the other part, you know.'

We set off in Jo's red BMW. At modest speed we turned into Surdiman Street. The street was crowded; the cars coming from the opposite direction were crawling even slower.

We were heading towards Kelapa Gading, to an elite housing complex. We finally arrived at eight thirty, easily finding house number

45 on PN Street. The guards at the entrance to the complex directed us past a cream-coloured house with a silver iron fence. Number 45 was the next house along.

'This is Michael's house,' said Jo, smiling. It was a large, modern building, luxurious in style, with many cars parked neatly outside in the front yard. Jo said that Michael was a German client of his, working for an electronics company whose advertising was handled by Jo's firm.

A security guard came up and opened the gate. There were already half a dozen prestige cars parked in front of us. I guessed their total value must have been billions of rupiah.

At the front terrace, we saw Michael in conversation with a man and a woman. As soon as he saw us, he immediately invited us to join them.

Michael introduced us to all the guests in the living room. There must have been about twenty people in the room, split evenly between men and women. Two of the male guests stood out. The first was Paul, about thirty-two years old, from Australia, and a twenty-nine-year-old German called John. I must admit I struggled to remember everybody's name.

However, I recognised most of them from the café scene in Jakarta. Michael, Paul and John were well recognised as they were acknowledged party animals.

Of all the women there, only a handful were Caucasian, most of them being local women. I was surprised that I recognised four of the local female guests.

Susan was twenty-four years old, tanned and stylish. She was often seen out and about in the elite cafés in Jakarta. In the evenings and at weekends, Susan usually went to the KT café in Central Jakarta.

Meanwhile we knew Maria as an escort from the BK karaoke bar in Surdiman Street. She was a long-haired blonde, about twenty-six, with what many men considered the perfect body. It could be said that Maria belonged to the top-ten ladies who were booked every night by rich men coming to BK.

The other two women, Diana and Noni, weren't new to us either. We recognized them well. We didn't know them intimately, but knew of them because of our long experience of the café and pub scene. Both of them were around twenty-five years old.

According to some friends who often joined us at the fashionable cafés, Diana and Noni were categorized as call girls who liked to take on underground jobs. They had two pimps: a woman and a transvestite. It was the two pimps that handled the girls' bookings, and Diana and Noni were frequently seen walking accompanied by one of their pimps.

Diana and Noni often spent the night in the cafés that were also visited by some white men, one of which was the new UT café, which had just been operating in the last six months in the Kuningan area. Previously, they were often seen at the JC café in a hotel in the Senayan district. So, I wasn't surprised to see them at the party. I guessed they must have been invited by one or two of the white men present that evening.

Most of the women were wearing dresses. All looked very sexy. Susan was wearing a blue V-cut dress, while Noni had draped her body in a very thin red dress, so that the outline of her bra and panties was clearly visible.

In the middle of the room was a long table, adorned with flowers, red wine and all manner of plates, napkins and utensils, as well as fresh fruit and a buffet for the guests. The rest of the living room was equally luxurious. The white marble floor was covered in part by a tasteful red carpet and a shiny, dark brown sofa. A crystal lamp on the side table provided the lighting. In one corner sat a large cupboard containing books and antiques. The cream-coloured walls were decorated with paintings and photographs. In another corner there was a television and hi-fi with a huge rack of CDs. A mini bar next to a small table and chairs rounded off the scene, complete with two bartenders standing by, ready to attend to the guests.

At nine fifteen we sat down to eat. The three courses were European in style. I had plenty of time to look around the room and observe closely all of the dining guests. Jo and I knew four of them already, but I didn't know the other seven women at the table. Maybe I'd seen them around before but I couldn't be sure. If I had seen them it would have been in a dim and hazy nightclub.

I happened to be sitting next to a girl wearing a pink dress. She was attractive, with shoulder-length curly hair. I discovered her name was Erna and that she was twenty-six. She was from Palembang and had worked for the last two years as a counter girl in a cosmetics boutique. She told me that she often spent her evenings and weekends in cafés, bars and discotheques. The cafés she mentioned were the ones frequented by Western men.

I looked at the seven unfamiliar girls and decided that they weren't that different from Maria, Noni, Diana or Susan. They were all good looking and sexy and took great care to smile a lot.

The easy conversations went on long into the warm night. Light laughter and music punctuated an enjoyable, convivial atmosphere. After a while, Michael invited us all over to the mini bar area, where disco music was now playing and a small laminated dance floor was beckoning.

The two waiters, who had been patiently lingering in the shadows, now swung into action, serving up all sorts of alcoholic beverages. I thought to myself that for Paul, Michael and John, all of this drinking was nothing new. All of them had a reputation for being good drinkers.

Our female guests were also getting into the swing of it, their drinks being replenished with great efficiency. The sounds of toasting, clinking glass, laughter and flirtatious jokes filled the air. The party was like a big happy family gathering. As I surveyed the scene—couples dancing and laughing, chatting and joking—it occurred to me that actually, this wasn't anything new. I could see the same thing any night in a Jakarta pub or nightclub. So what made tonight any different?

Well, I was about to find out. The main course of the evening was not in fact, the delicious rib steak, but something else entirely.

Almost imperceptibly the mood changed as the girls removed their evening gowns. Maria, Susan, Noni and Diana, as well as the others, were now wearing just bras and knickers. The laughter was now replaced by flirtatious giggling, as the girls moved their bodies to an erotic rhythm in keeping with the music. The party was getting hotter as the time approached eleven. The girls' underwear had now disappeared. We stared in amazement as the girls swayed and turned, moving their beautiful curves to the beat of the night.

Paul and Jo were dancing amongst the girls, bumping their bodies up to the naked flesh gyrating before them. They laughed and joked with each other, the alcohol clearly relieving them of any inhibitions.

The sweet mix of alcohol and sweat was very strong. Some of the female guests were now just watching the party in a daze. It felt like the evening would continue for ever. In fact, the striptease dancing was just the opening act. Michael, our host, announced that his guests could 'execute' one of the girls if he wanted to!

Some men, who had been excited by alcoholic drinks and the luscious dances, did not let this chance pass them by. John, for example, directly nudged one of the girls, I think her name was Lusi, and took her to the first floor.

Michael laughed to himself as Jo and I shook our heads in wonderment. It was of course now obvious that Michael had provided these girls and the rooms for his guests. The girls weren't just dancers, but also call girls, or 'chickens', as prostitutes are frequently called in much of Southeast Asia. The term 'chicken night' was used informally to describe the evening that I had witnessed—an opportunity to dance the night away, drink and have fun in the company of beautiful girls and then, crucially, to satisfy one's carnal desires.

On the way home Jo and I laughed together as we recalled our evening. We tried not to think too deeply about what this service was all about. This wasn't really about looking for a long-term spouse; it was about men satisfying their lustful desires while having a whole lot of fun.

No Hands Service

While the NHS in the United Kingdom is frequently criticized for the decreasing quality of its national healthcare, the NHS in Jakarta is a thriving practice dedicated to improving the quality of life of the city's male residents. Albeit behind closed doors and at a steep price.

The many new ways to satiate a man's desire are always innovative and challenging. The events are prepared thoroughly and marketed strongly, much like any other product in a competitive marketplace. Jakarta has seen squeals on wheels, casino nights and naked parties and even though the main attraction is always the same thing—the act of sex—a new service had successfully emerged in recent years called NHS, or No Hands Service.

When I heard about NHS for the first time I must admit I didn't really know what was involved. My friend, who worked as a general manager at TW, a karaoke pub in the Mangga Dua district, first told me of this new phenomenon. Michael, a thirty-two-year-old single guy, was rather plump and liked to frequent the night entertainment venues in Jakarta.

As usual, it was only a casual talk in the beginning. I first met Michael at the MT café in Surdiman. In our next meeting, Michael, who was born in Surabaya, began talking more freely and bluntly. One thing that he always talked about was his adventures in tracking the nightlife in Jakarta. So when he mentioned a karaoke pub, which offered a No Hands Service, I was very curious.

Such a term was still a little strange in the afterdark vocabulary of Jakarta. When I admitted to Michael that I knew nothing about NHS, he explained that it was a new type of service that had only been operating formally in the last one year.

Well, I thought I shouldn't let the chance pass me by to see this for myself. I made a date to meet with Michael on a Friday evening at PC café, which was situated at SP Mall, in South Jakarta. Michael came with his friend, Joseph, a close friend and colleague.

It was eight thirty in the evening. After only fifteen minutes of us meeting, Michael suggested we set off. We took my black Jeep Wrangler, heading towards the centre of the city. As is usual in Jakarta the traffic was bad, indeed the cars coming the other way seemed to be gridlocked. We turned into GT Street and entered TH Street in Central Jakarta. I drove slowly up to the carpark of a shopping mall the locals called SP, which was situated just off the main high street in Central Jakarta.

It was about nine fifteen when we locked the car and headed for the lift. We got out on the fifteenth floor and entered the venue: a one-stop discotheque, restaurant and karaoke bar in a cavernous room that was about 500 metres square. The place was popularly known as NW.

Music blasted from speakers in all four corners of the room. The DJ was playing RnB, trance and acid jazz. Amidst bright shining lights, the guests danced and drank, chatted and laughed with each other. The discotheque was in the middle of the room whereas the restaurant was over in the right-hand corner. We bypassed both and headed to the reception area where two ladies in dark blue blazers met us.

Michael had already reserved a room.

'It's always full here. If I hadn't reserved a spot, we'd have been put on a waiting list,' he said.

A girl led us to our room. Walking down the corridor I could see a row of rooms. In front of each door a woman was standing by. I could hear music coming softly from each room. We were guided to a door on which was written Royal Suite, like you might see in a smart hotel.

The Royal Suite was located at the end of the row of rooms, next to four other VIP rooms. The suite was about twelve metres across and could accommodate about fifteen to twenty guests. Usually, it was in a room like this that wealthy executives might hold a private party. It could be held just for fun, or to entertain or serve clients with a meal, to celebrate a birthday or even to hold a bachelor party.

Inside the room I could see three cream sofas, a metallic black table and two large televisions. The walls were pink, adorned by three abstract paintings of women. There was a comfortable, luxurious feel to the place. The air conditioning added a welcome chill to the air.

Next to one of the televisions was a locked cupboard containing many types of drinks and glasses. Beyond the cupboard was a bedroom equipped with a spring bed and an en-suite bathroom. A colourful quilt adorned the bed along with some pillows and cushions. Above the bed a light bulb shone dimly.

I took a seat and ordered some food and drink. From the entrance door a woman appeared. She looked like an office worker, dressed in a miniskirt with a cream shirt and blue blazer. The woman, who I knew as one of the mammies at NW, asked me to choose one of the girls from her collection. It appeared that as a regular, Michael had already chosen his girl.

'I've just booked Vita and Dina. Can you ask them to come over here?' said Michael to the mammy. She nodded and quickly disappeared behind the door.

While we were waiting for the two escorts, I decided to partake in some karaoke. On the table in front of me were three song lists containing Indonesian, Western and Mandarin songs. I had sung along to a couple of tracks when Vita and Dina, accompanied by the mammy, walked into the room.

I immediately thought to myself that Michael's choice was indeed very good. Both girls were young and pretty.

Without saying anything, they came over and sat near us. They invited us all to sing together, as they slowly attached their bodies to ours. Vita was getting intimate with Michael, while Joseph was amorous with Dina. Myself? Well, don't be surprised, it was enough for me to observe the party!

Both couples then performed a duet, song by song. I sensed that the singing was really just a sideshow as I watched the couples laughing and rubbing up against each other. The image of two couples absorbed in each other looked for the entire world like any date you might see on a regular evening out.

'Would you like something a bit hotter? You don't want to sing all night do you?' asked Vita mischievously.

Dina smiled temptingly as Vita said this.

As a regular visitor to NW, Michael clearly knew what she meant. He had tried the 'hot service' before.

While grabbing some fresh fruit from the table, Vita quickly got up from her seat. She then stepped forward, followed by Dina. The music changed to a pounding, house-mania type of music. On the television the karaoke was replaced by pictures of dancers who were undulating sexily, and stripping for the camera.

Vita and Dina were also moving their bodies like the white girls on the TV screen. Their moves weren't exactly the same of course, but their dancing was certainly erotic. As if in a contest, they seemed to be competing with the girls on the TV.

The focus now shifted as Vita and Dina also began to remove their clothes. Their slow dancing continued as they approached Michael and Joseph, trying to seduce them.

This went on for a little while until Vita and Dina now moved closer to each other. Much closer. Vita spoke.

'Now it's my turn. I'm the queen. No hands service, OK? Just sit back and don't say anything,' she said softly, smiling as she did so.

Michael poured himself a Hennessy Cognac and gulped it down quickly. Joseph did the same.

Soon after Michael put down his glass, Vita started to taunt him, as did Dina with Joseph. Aggressively, they began taking off Michael and Joseph's clothes, while the music continued to play loudly. The activities in the VIP room changed into a very hot and ravishing party, sizzling with deadly lust.

Michael and Joseph were now as still as statues. They were not allowed to react to the girls. These were the rules. They were only allowed to enjoy and feel what the girls were doing, no more than that.

This seemed like an unfair battle to me, what with two aggressive girls whose sexy movements could make a man surrender and yet they were unable to do anything to change their fate.

Like in a stage show, Vita put slices of fresh fruit on Michael's body. The beautiful Vita was now using her man's body as a dining table. This scene reminded me of sashimi sex, something only served up by special escort girls in select VIP karaoke bars.

In the other corner, Dina, who would also undoubtedly get top marks for her beauty, was now spraying red wine onto Joseph's body. She rubbed in the wine with her tongue and lips. I could only imagine how sensual and erotic this must have felt to Joseph.

This was without doubt an original new service. I was intrigued as to what new concept the sex entertainment scene could conjure up after this one.

At the end of the party Michael and Joseph handed over hundreds of thousands of rupiah. I didn't know exactly how much, but I was sure that the party had ended with a big smile and much wheezing laughter.

Now I finally understood what No Hands Service meant. This was basically a submissive service where the man was powerless to react to the actions of a sexy girl. Of course the end result was the same: sex, but at least this was a little different and more challenging for the customer. The spices and recipes if you like, were different, which made it more enticing to the lustful male.

Here at least, it was the NHS package that had become the main product on offer. There were around thirty girls available to serve their guests, whether it be a striptease, sashimi or three-in-one service. The escort girls were displayed in a special open room but the mammy organized everything, from the booking to the girl selection.

On the way out, I took a look around. I met a guy called Antoni who asked me to join him for a moment while we ate the leftovers of the party food. Antoni talked a lot about the awesomeness of NHS, which, according to him, could not be found in other entertainment venues.

'You know, this one is excellent,' said Antoni.

The striptease and sashimi services weren't new to Antoni, who had sampled them before, but this NHS service was a new idea. Antoni had tried it twice now.

'It would be much more exciting if they were combined into one service—striptease, sashimi and NHS. The combination is terrific,' Antoni said.

Michael had certainly proved this. However, it didn't come cheap to get the three-in-one service. If a guest ordered a VIP room, for example, the minimum duration was for three hours, and it was Rp125,000 (US$12) per hour. Meanwhile, a striptease cost Rp500,000 (US$50) and sashimi cost Rp750,000 (US$75). The most expensive of all was the NHS package. Just imagine, if a guest ordered such a super hot service, he would have to pay Rp1 million (US$100) for it!

I remembered Michael groping around in his pocket when settling up with the cashier. He took out some fifty-thousand-denomination notes, which he called his greased-palm money.

'These extras really help. When you come here the next time the service will be much better. And hotter!' Joseph had said, laughing.

It was nearly one in the morning when I left the party room. Vita and Dina had disappeared fifteen minutes earlier. Along the corridor of the room, I could still hear music, laughter and contented sighs.

I imagined what must have been going on inside these rooms. A group of men might be falling into the arms of escort girls while singing, or maybe they were now at the mercy of the NHS practitioners. These rich men would no doubt be drowning in wine, warmth and lustful pleasure, their minds and bodies being lulled into a soporific state of near nirvana.

Sashimi Sex

For customers with jaded palates, the only solution is to experience the raw sensual flavours of sashimi sex. Available on leading menus in Jakarta and Bali.

One February day, my friend and fellow journalist, who also did infotainment programmes on a private television network, and I, attended the birthday party of a famous singer and movie actor, known as SM. We'd met him some time back in a café in Taman Ria Senayan.

The party wasn't actually open to journalists, it was for specially invited guests only. I was among the invitees because I knew SM socially. Among the other guests were artists, producers and various successful young executives who of course had plenty of money and who loved to go out at night.

I was introduced by SM to one of the young executives at the party. He was Hans, a thirty-two-year-old man, who worked as an account director for a famous Japanese electronics company. While enjoying all kinds of special drinks that were on offer, we were soon having an animated discussion about the nightlife in Jakarta. At first our conversation was limited to the young people who frequented the pubs, clubs and cafés in Jakarta, but then our stories progressed to the escort ladies and the various services they provided.

As a wealthy man, Hans belonged to the crowd who could afford to entertain themselves frequently and in style. He told me that after he finished work he often liked to go into the town and relax in the cafés and bars while drinking beer or red wine. On other occasions he hosted his business clients by offering them a 'road show' of several entertainment options; from the bars, which were just for fun, to the places that offered more obvious sexual enticements.

As a man who knew the after dark scene well, Hans had experienced many diverse places offering equally diverse special packages for their guests. The one service that he found particularly special though was the unusual sashimi menu.

It was unusual because the sashimi, a Japanese delicacy of sliced raw seafood, was not served on a tray with chopsticks but was presented on the naked body of a beautiful, sensual girl.

Hans had thought he'd seen it all before but even he didn't quite understand why this sashimi package was proving so popular. Those who were interested in it were certainly rich men. They had to be because the asking price for this service ran into millions of rupiah.

I was reminded of what Dr Bambang Sukamto, a program officer in an Indonesian clinic, had said when I had interviewed him. His assertion was that whatever at first seemed like a deviation from the prevailing norms, would eventually, given time, become quite commonplace and acceptable. Dr Bambang saw sashimi sex in this way.

'Besides achieving a pleasure from food, someone can also get sexual satisfaction through an erotic view of a woman's body,' he said.

What was certain was that the package of sashimi sex was now offered by a number of places that wanted to attract as many guests as possible and drain their money by offering them a service that was somewhat unconventional.

Sex is indeed rich in variation. And it's this variety that is used by some places to offer up new menus of sexual service. So, when bored with striptease dances, or fed up with going to massage parlours, sashimi sex becomes a new option for the palate.

Striptease can easily be found in many entertainment places in the big cities of Jakarta and Surabaya, not to mention the massage parlours which offer short-time sex and a variety of extras that are widely spread throughout Indonesia's larger cities like Bandung, Medan and Batam.

But not many places offer sashimi sex.

Imagine a very beautiful girl with creamy skin lying naked on a table with pieces of sashimi arranged delicately over her body. Two or three men are dancing around her supine figure, leaning in to pick off the pieces of seafood with their mouths.

'You know, sex is rich with artistic images, and it's in such art that the beauty and pleasure lie,' joked Hans.

Curious to see the real sashimi action, I made a date with Hans. On the agreed day, we met in the lobby of a five-star hotel in Surdiman Street. Because the traffic in Jakarta has no compromise in the afternoons, we arranged to meet at about seven in the evening.

'Just relax, the place is not far from here. Let's have some coffee first. Anyway, I've booked,' said Hans, who was wearing jeans and a Giorgio Armani T-shirt. After relaxing for some minutes while enjoying a cup of coffee, we left for the location in Hans's BMW.

Upon entering Thamrin Street, we had to slow down to no faster than sixty kilometres per hour. After passing some traffic lights, we crawled along the slow lane for about twenty-five metres, until turning to face one of the doors of a tower block. I didn't ask much, Hans seemed to know where he was going.

Having parked the car round the back we took the lift almost to the top of the building, alighting on the eighth of ten floors.

It was ten to eight when we reached the reception desk. A female receptionist welcomed us, she had short hair and was wearing a black jacket with a white shirt and a knee-length skirt. She introduced herself as Susan.

'Good Evening Hans, we have prepared a room for you,' she said with a beautiful smile.

So far Hans seemed to be well recognized at the NZ club. Susan was very friendly in a professional but familiar way.

'Would you like the usual, sir? Or maybe you want to try a new product?' she asked cheekily.

'OK, that's a good idea. Can you take her straight to my room?' replied Hans quickly.

We were taken immediately to a waiting room. The lamps cast a dim light around us and from another room we could hear the soft laughter of a woman.

'That's a special room for the escort ladies,' whispered Hans.

I looked at this room with its door slightly ajar and could see that Hans was right. Some girls were going in and coming out in turn.

The room in which we sat was quite small. It was equipped with a sofa and a screen. Next to the screen was a square table made of alabaster on which a lamp stood.

'Would you like me to call her now, Hans?' asked Susan.

Hans then approached her.

'If you have no new stock, you'd better provide us with the ones we are familiar with. Wati and Yeni would be fine. I've just booked both of them,' he said.

Susan then left us. While waiting for our order the background music switched to slow, romantic songs. Hans was relaxed, humming along to the music. Ten minutes later Susan came back with two gorgeous girls. After delivering our order, Susan left the four of us alone.

It seemed that the girls were indeed Wati and Yeni. Wati had curly, shoulder-length hair and a fair complexion. She was wearing a flowered shirt, a miniskirt and a black jacket. Meanwhile Yeni had quite long straight hair, creamy skin and a prominent nose. She was taller than Wati and was wearing a V-shaped dress.

Hans was immediately at ease with the girls and introduced them to me. I tried to make myself comfortable with them, although I felt a little awkward as we all made small talk. As the drinks flowed, we all sang along to the karaoke.

'Would you like us to begin the show now, babe?' asked Yeni, who was by now hanging leisurely from Hans's shoulders.

'OK, that's fine. You know my friend here can't wait to watch it,' Hans said, as he looked at me. Wati, who was sitting next to me, just smiled. She then got up and spoke.

'Let me order the food first.'

She pressed a button on the table and a waitress appeared. It seemed like only moments later that the sashimi was served.

Meanwhile, as a television screen showed images of some sexy girls undulating to the rhythm of some pulsating music, Wati and Yeni swung into action. They were soon clambering onto the alabaster table and pulling off their clothes piece by piece until they were completely naked. Then they slowly and suggestively picked up pieces of sashimi with their thumb and forefinger and placed them onto their gorgeous sexy bodies.

For a few minutes, they swayed their bodies sensually to the music. I just kept silent, waiting for Hans's reaction. Although he was smiling cheerfully, I knew nothing of what he had in mind.

'Come on, don't be shy. Eat the sashimi,' shouted Hans, while looking at me.

Frankly speaking, I didn't know what to do when faced with two naked girls moving so sensually. The sashimi only added to the excitement.

I didn't react at all until Hans took control of the situation. At first, he took a pair of chopsticks from the table. With his fingers he picked up some sashimi from a nearby body part and popped it into his mouth. I wasn't sure why Hans had picked up the chopsticks because he then put them back down and moved his mouth closer to Yeni's naked body.

Her luscious skin was now one large plate! Hans dived in and began to devour the sashimi. I shook my head in amazement—there was always something new to discover in Jakarta—then followed suit.

NZ was first and foremost a karaoke joint. It had been offering the sashimi package for more than four years, but this was only for certain people. NZ was, like other types of karaoke centres in Jakarta, open for everyone, but in terms of the package of sashimi sex, not all of the guests could partake.

Most venues used to be more selective as to who could sample the sashimi service, but now it seemed that this service was available to anyone with money. Not all the escort girls, however, offered sashimi sex, so the waitresses started giving coded signals to the new guests to let them know who was available. This wasn't necessary for people like Hans of course, who knew all the girls very well by now.

Once the guests had made the decision to go with the escort girls for sashimi sex, they just waited in the karaoke room and then ordered their food from a waitress. It didn't have to be sashimi; some sliced fresh fruit would do just as well.

A rival sashimi venue came onto the scene in the late nineties, offering a restaurant and disco as well as karaoke. It was called SN and was on the fourteenth floor of a shopping center in the Thamrin district of Central Jakarta.

SN provided three packages—all slightly different and this became its unique selling point. Besides sashimi sex, which attracted a lot of guests, there were two other types of service, namely the striptease dance and a package of NHS.

The sashimi sex service seemed to be no different to the one offered by NZ, but because SN had been operating for less than two years it was very selective in offering the service to its guests. It was mainly a case of offering it as a premium to its respected guests only.

To manage the sashimi girls, SN employed several mammies or mamasans. The mammies supervised at least fifty ladies, classifying them into groups, as not all of them could give sashimi sex to the guests.

When the guests wanted to sample sashimi sex, the mammies would then gather some suitably trained girls and send them directly to the karaoke room. Here the guests chose whomever they liked, but if they couldn't find the girl they were after, the mammies would call in the next group until the guests were satisfied.

The karaoke room at SN was a bit larger than the one at NZ. The interior design was quite different from the interior design at NZ, taking a very modern approach, which was understandable because SN was still new and it needed to attract patrons. SN was replete with a long sofa and wide table but it didn't use a projector screen, rather it provided a 29-inch television.

The emergence of SN with its new packages was helping to make sashimi sex ever more popular. Although not many men knew of the sex service, for night stalkers the sashimi package at NZ and SN was a hit. There were a lot of young executives who had been hunting for just this kind of sex service. Naturally, a lot of Japanese men had become loyal sashimi-sex customers.

The cost? It was expensive indeed, because for one sitting the guests had to pay Rp1 million (US$100). The cost was basically the same at both NZ and SN, although the price didn't include the karaoke room where the minimum booking time was three hours, with a fee of Rp125,000 (US$12) per hour.

The Rp1 million price was the only one quoted on the billing list. This was for one show only, it was understood that the girls would be expecting tips if their guests wished to take things any further. For each additional course, the girls would be expecting around Rp200,000 (US$20), which begs the question: just how much would a hungry man have to spend to get the complete package of sashimi sex?

It would probably come to about Rp3 million (US$300), but this didn't seem to deter men (in a country where the average per capita GNP is approximately US$800 per year). Hans had told me that it wasn't really to do with how much it cost, more that it was a case of satisfying desires because one had the freedom to do so.

Sashimi sex had not been monopolized by Jakarta. Bali also offered it, although the form it took there was a little different. Among the hundreds of bars and discotheques in the Kuta, Legian and Seminyak areas there was one place providing its guests with what it called a Sashimi Girl Dance.

On a bar table, three girls wearing bikinis would dance while simultaneously offering sashimi which was distributed over their bodies. I viewed this at NT's club in the Legian area, about one month after I had witnessed the sashimi sex at NZ in Jakarta. I saw dozens of men standing hungrily near this bar table, eagerly waiting for and clearly welcoming the sashimi. It was one thirty in the morning and by now the dancers were soaked with sweat. Suddenly they removed their bikini tops and threw them into the crowd.

Whichever lucky man caught a flying bikini was invited to dance along with the girls. As the night progressed, everyone was being whipped up into a frenzy of excitement as time and again the women threw their bikinis into the crowd. It seems that Bali is Bali and Jakarta is Jakarta!

The sashimi girls in Bali seemed to be more like striptease dancers although the men still got to nibble the seafood from off their bodies if they'd managed to catch the bikinis being thrown at them.

'It's only a matter of appearance and style when it comes to serving the guests. Principally, the girls and the sashimi are the same, aren't they?' Hans had commented when I talked to him about the sashimi girls in Bali.

NT's was more of a members' club and usually held special events where the sashimi dancing would take place. It wasn't offered to all the guests, just the members. In order to be a member you had to pay Rp7 million (US$700) for the regular class and Rp10 million (US$1000) for the VIP class. Each class was provided with different facilities. For the regular class, for example, on a special event, every member got a table with four chairs and a bottle of Black Label whiskey. In order to be able to have an escort lady sit with them, a guest had to pay Rp500,000 (US$50). VIP guests didn't need to pay any extra to for an escort lady to accompany them for an evening. There was no on-the-spot sex service at NT's but the VIP guests were allowed to book the girls to be taken out, although they would then have to pay Rp1 million (US$100).

Besides NT'S there was also a karaoke centre in Denpasar called KSA, which also offered a sashimi girl service for its members. It provided the usual karaoke room but also special extra rooms. By paying Rp500,000 (US$50) a member could get a bedroom with a television and video. Here the guest had free reign with the sashimi girl and would pay her directly for her services.

It was said that the sashimi girls at KSA were wilder and sexier than elsewhere. Besides being famous for their exciting dancing, they were also known for being like hungry tigers in bed! They had a reputation for being ready to pounce on their prey with no mercy.

Unfortunately, after both Bali bomb blast tragedies, the entertainment scene in Bali dropped considerably but is sure to bounce back.

Club 99

For the very wealthy and the very well known, discretion is paramount. At this seemingly innocuous dinner club, with its surprisingly attractive waitresses, sex is definitely not on the menu. But a quiet word in a waitress's ear is all that is needed to set a date for a future rendezvous.

An ordinary-looking white house from the outside, the low-key residence offers no clues as to what actually goes on inside. With a tall fence and high windows, it resembles any other massive house in Pondok Indah.

Located on the busy LB street in Central Jakarta, not far from a market and shopping centre, the house looks deserted by day. Only three cars are parked in the lot, which is large enough to accommodate a dozen or more vehicles.

This scene however changes when night falls. Scores of people, men and women alike, descend on the property, and the luxury cars lining the street around the driveway give a clue as to the identity of the occupants.

A friend of mine had been telling me about this curious place and given that he had many contacts, it had surprised him that he didn't know more about it. Ardi was a thirty-year-old assistant to the marketing director of a heavy-equipment company.

As we played billiards in a bar, Ardi explained that he was a real lover of the night scene in Jakarta, not to mention in the other big cities like Surabaya, Bandung and Medan. He felt that he was experienced in visiting all the different places on offer, so when he first heard of Club 99 he was a little dismayed he didn't know more about it.

His friends had told him of the stunningly sexy girls who were waitresses there, and that all the guests travelled to Club 99 in luxury cars. This was enough to get Ardi's attention, he had to know more!

As luck would have it, a business friend of Ardi's had recently invited him along to have dinner at the club. Pram was a thirty-two-year-old project director in a similar industry to Ardi. The story was that Pram wanted to treat Ardi after the successful signing of a business contract.

So it was that one Friday evening, Ardi invited me to meet up at BG café after work. It was a small café, which could only accommodate about a hundred people, so it was soon bustling inside. Shortly after we arrived, Pram turned up alone.

At about eight we left the café and set off in search of Club 99. Pram drove his Mercedes while Ardi and I followed in Ardi's car. We passed Surdiman Street, which was as busy as usual, then, after going through three sets of lights, we entered South Jakarta. From a large intersection we turned off into LB street, which was home to several restaurants and a plaza.

This was a lively street. We could see hordes of pretty young things laughing and joking outside the busy restaurants and food stalls. We watched Pram park his Mercedes a few yards away then parked up behind him. It seemed that we'd stopped in front of a house whose number wasn't clear. There was nothing there to tell us where we were.

So this was Club 99. It didn't look much. Well, it just looked like a perfectly normal, presentable urban dwelling. The lights were on inside but we couldn't see people yet. We knew it was occupied though due to the dozen or so luxury cars in the driveway.

What was actually happening inside? Pram, who had knocked on the door moments earlier, invited us to come in. The teak door opened to reveal a girl wearing a very short miniskirt and black shirt, with a flowery scarf draped around her neck. She welcomed us inside.

We'd moved no more than a few feet when another similarly dressed girl appeared.

'The table is ready sir. It's over there near the bar,' she said.

The strain of music was barely audible over the chatter inside. Almost all of the tables were occupied, and the guests were clearly having a good time. Laughter and a sense of fun filled the air.

Some people came up and said hello to Pram. It seemed that most of the people appeared to be familiar with each other.

'This is a private club. Only members and guests are allowed to come here,' said Pram.

A waitress then approached our table and offered us the menus. There were various kinds of cuisine offered such as Indonesian, European and Chinese. But the most popular offering was Japanese. The prices on the menu were about the same as those in a five-star hotel, maybe even a bit higher.

We observed the other guests. They all had much in common: they were well dressed, stylish and their general air and mannerisms gave off a comfortable confidence that could only come from being contented with what life was offering them.

I recognised some of the guests as being prominent local figures. Let's take BO for example, who was a famous young executive who had a construction company and a string of restaurants. Another was RF, the son of a Chinese tycoon, who was also well known because he had a special relationship with a beautiful actress. Not far from our table were various other famous young men from all sorts of professions. Most of them seemed to be attached to a sexy young waitress.

'You know, it's expensive to become a member. And it's not easy, either,' said Pram all of a sudden, disturbing our concentration.

Pram's remark made us enquire further. It was said that in order to become a member, someone had to pay more or less Rp5 million (US$500) for a silver card and Rp10 million (US$1000) for the gold card. Additionally, in order to become a member, prospective members had to be proposed by an existing member.

'I became a member just because I knew FT quite well. You know FT, the famous lawyer, don't you?' continued Pram, smiling.

The two types of card represented different types of service. A member who had the gold card, for instance, could attend every event that was held—such as the sexy-women, wild-girl and hot-dancer parties—without paying any extra money. Silver-card holders had to pay an extra charge of up to fifty percent. The parties frequently held at Club 99 were said to be wild and they all had hot themes. It was not too unlike the live shows held in special rooms in some entertainment venues in Jakarta.

'The parties are always sensational; really hot,' said Pram as he recalled some of the previous events at Club 99.

One week before, said Pram, they held a Wet Party where five sexy girls wore nothing but thin, and soon transparent, wet T-shirts. Usually, such an event was held once a month.

For nearly two hours we had been ceaselessly observing tens of waitresses who were walking back and forth to serve the guests from table to table. It was fantastic, the girls were wearing black uniforms and yet were still beautiful and sexy.

'Not one is bad, right? That's the outstanding feature of Club 99. All of the waitresses are beautiful,' said Pram, smiling.

'If you are finished, the relaxation room is ready on the first floor, sir,' whispered a waitress.

It seemed that the main attraction of Club 99 was indeed its waitresses.

We were invited to go up to the first floor by taking the stairs. I could still hear the soft music reverberating around the room.

A door was opened for us. We must have all wondered what was coming next. In fact, there were some private rooms, which were set side by side on the first floor. A waitress took us to Room 9. There was no nameplate stuck to the door as you might see on the doors of some pubs or karaoke joints. The rooms were only named Room 1, 2, 3 and so on. Our room was right at the end of the row.

After walking some steps forward we heard indistinct sighs of laughter, and pampering voices from somewhere inside the room. Pram only winked at us and asked us to keep on walking. It was nothing, he said.

'They were probably just joking while pinching each other, ha ha ...' jested Pram, as we continued walking.

Room 9 was a simple room with a long sofa and a table. It was equipped with other facilities such as a television and VCR. Its floor was covered with a dark blue carpet. On the table were various kinds of fresh fruit like apples, grapes, oranges, pears, and four bottles of white and red wine.

'I ordered all of these things before we left. I booked in advance,' said Pram.

There was no operator as was usually the case in a karaoke room. A collection of CDs and VCDs was neatly arranged near the television. Pram, who had been accustomed to the service at Club 99, immediately turned on the television and played a selection of Lionel Richie songs.

'The girls you've ordered will be here in a few minutes, sir,' said the girl who had accompanied us to the room. She then retreated and disappeared behind the door.

After enjoying the fruit and some tunes, we heard a knock at the door. Three waitresses wearing black uniforms with miniskirts and scarves around their necks entered the room in single file. Their smiles and welcome greeting made us all feel very relaxed.

'Good evening Mr Pram,' they said one by one.

Pram then invited them to join us on the sofa. Without being asked the three girls began to serve us. They weren't giving us extra service like voluptuous dancing or anything like that. Not at all. They acted exactly like real waitresses. First of all, they offered us some wine. When we wanted to change the music, they then asked us what songs we liked, after which they changed the music.

Our brief acquaintance didn't seem to be a stumbling block. The girls behaved as if they'd known us for a long time. Pram might have known the three girls because as a member who had a gold card, his face was well recognised in the place. But for Ardi and myself, it was quite strange.

They served us politely, even though they sometimes behaved rather intimately. In a few minutes, the relaxation room had indeed become relaxing. A place for us to enjoy our leisure accompanied by some beautiful girls, being served and treated like kings.

When the king wanted to eat a piece of pear and touch the waitress's soft and cute chin, the girl would happily oblige. When the king wanted to be pampered with a smile and an intimate embrace, the girls would quickly move closer to him. Everything was possible except one thing: sex. If a guest requested sex, the girls would politely and gently refuse by kissing the guest.

'Sorry, we don't do it here, OK?'

As I said earlier, the girls were truly beautiful with great figures. They couldn't have been more than about twenty-seven years old. From their make-up and the way they spoke and behaved, it was clear that they'd been well trained for the job. It wasn't surprising really that the girls were well groomed considering their clients were so rich and no doubt accustomed to the very best.

I wondered how satisfied the guests were though, without any sexual gratification. Especially for the price. Pram had explained to us that for one waitress, he had to spend Rp500,000 (US$50). That excluded the money spent on food, drinks and the use of the place. For Rp500,000, the waitress was still just a waitress, albeit a very devoted and sexy one. Admittedly also a waitress who could be kissed, embraced and fondled to a guest's content, but still there was no sex service.

I asked Intan about the 'service plus'. Intan was a waitress with shining eyes, creamy skin and shoulder-length hair. She was twenty-four years old and drop-dead gorgeous.

'It can be arranged. But not here. We can make a date.'

A short answer, and one that meant 'yes'.

Finally we realized how it all worked. Club 99 had made the waitresses its unique selling point. It was in the club that a subtle love rendezvous could be negotiated. A place where people set a discreet date, which in the end led simply to another sex transaction.

For the very wealthy and the very well known, who could not be seen entering other less salubrious venues, this club provided a discreet setting where all that was required was for the man to whisper a few words. Such and such a time in such and such a hotel, and the deal could be worth Rp1, 2 or 3 million (US$100 to 300) for the night.

Drive Thru' Sex

Convenience seems to be the unique selling point of this 'drive thru' establishment. And a money-spinner it is too. Simply drive up, order, pay and take away.

The sound of pandering voices and soft laughter drifted out from the medium-sized room. A dozen pretty girls showed coy, flirtatious smiles as a middle-aged woman chatted intimately to two men in casual clothes, who were simultaneously scanning the room.

The mens' eyes were keenly observing twelve women dressed in tight clothes. Most of them were still young, around twenty to twenty-five years old. At a glance, they looked like models displaying their make-up and clothing. But one thing was for sure: they showed off as much skin as they could, because these attractive young women were here to quench the love thirst of two men present.

It was already eight thirty but the two guests had yet to make a decision. The lady of the house asked the twelve young women to leave the room. In the next moment, from a doorway covered by a bright red curtain, that led to an inner room, appeared another ten girls. They were as pretty as the previous batch. With their make-up they looked ravishing—enticing lipstick and alluring perfumes.

The two guests sat relaxed while observing the girls. One of them, a thirty-year-old man, wore a black shirt and his hair was well groomed.

His companion, however, was dressed in casual clothes: a polo shirt and jeans. He looked to be in his early thirties, and appeared confused and greedy, with a lecherous eye looking as if he might pounce on and swallow the girls. His behaviour made us uncomfortable; he was acting like a clumsy rhinoceros.

A waitress served drinks. The man in the black shirt indicated his choice: a girl with shoulder-length hair, red lipstick and a long, tight T-shirt. Meanwhile, the man wearing casual clothes chose a girl in a shiny black skirt and her hair in a bun.

The chosen girls then said goodbye and left the room briefly to gather their bags. The mamasan handled the payments efficiently, and as soon as the girls came back the men were ready to go. Where they were taking them I couldn't be sure, but I had a good idea.

This was the infamous house Number 20, a house that was known to provide beautiful girls for special love orders. The house was frequently the subject of café gossip all over Jakarta. Gossiping about call girls is nothing new. Such girls can easily be seen in discotheques, cafés, bars and pubs. We were often reminded of their presence by the matchmakers who can be seen wandering amongst guests in many entertainment places. But the girls of Number 20 seemed to have become a hot topic in the past few months.

'They're stylish and beautiful. Pay on the spot, and you can take them out. The rest is up to you,' said one of my friends, Ardian, a sociable man prone to wasting his money, despite the fact his restaurant business wasn't as successful as he'd like.

I was very curious, so together with two young executives who'd just attended a birthday party with me in a café, I tried to find the house. My two friends, Rudy, twenty-eight years old, and Andre, thirty, worked in the same company, an export–import company trading in spare car parts. They weren't newcomers to the night scene, in fact they claimed that they'd even been to the love house before.

It wasn't difficult to find house Number 20. Previously, it was located in SW Street, not far from the traffic lights at a big T-junction connecting Mangga Besar, Hayam Wuruk and Mangga Dua. But now it was situated at Taman Sari, in the Mangga Besar area. Actually it wasn't very far from the original location.

During the daytime, the area around the house was very crowded. This was because Taman Sari is full of shops and food stalls. Most of the places were open twenty-four hours. Not to mention the activities of love-peddling girls, soliciting sex on the street, who were waiting for men driving by in their cars.

Around five cars were parked in front of the house in question. The parking lot wasn't very wide; at the most it could accommodate ten or twelve cars. Two parking attendants were there to watch over the cars belonging to the guests.

The house was pretty big, not less than thirty by thirty metres. Its living room was fairly sizeable and was equipped with a table and some chairs, a television and an attached bathroom. A middle-aged woman, who was in fact the mammy of the house, welcomed us politely. The house had no special interior decor but the air conditioning made the room pleasantly cool. On the wall were some paintings and posters. Indonesian and foreign lifestyle magazines were arranged neatly on the table.

The magazines mostly contained photos of sexy girls—no *Playboy* or *Penthouse* though. There were also some other local magazines and tabloid newspapers. A 24-inch television was relaying the programs of a domestic television channel.

Besides us, there were another three men in the living room. Some minutes later, the three guys left, followed by three extremely cute girls. We were indifferent, watching them pass through the living room. Rudy and Andre were having a chat with the mamasan, Mammy Tety.

It seemed that Rudy and Andre were well known in the love house.

Mammy Tety teased them because they hadn't been there for a long time. She told them gently that there were some new collections.

'The girls are still very young and beautiful. I guarantee you, they are great,' she said.

Wow, she treats the girls like a product, I thought to myself.

But Mammy Tety was right. In the next moment she came back to us with five girls in tow. She asked them to take a seat in a row, on dark blue chairs, then announced their names one by one.

The five girls introduced to us were Karin, Ana, Indah, Sonya and Besty. All of them were above average. Karin and Sonya were particularly beautiful. Both of them exuded a raw sex appeal, which was somehow more pronounced than Indah, Ana, and Besty's. According to Mammy Tety, they ranked in the top ten at Number 20.

'Hey, you know, these girls are part of our best new collection. For special guests only,' said Mammy Tety.

Such a sales spiel was probably a standard line to all male guests at the house, but according to Andre, the girls certainly were newcomers. When seeing Karin and Sonya for the first time, Andre had said to me that these girls were really fresh and exciting.

'Mammy, your collections are not bad,' said Andre in understated fashion, since all mammies will praise their protégés without exception.

The girls smiled appreciatively when they heard Andre say this. I looked at their clothes. Most of them were wearing miniskirts, showing their sexy legs. Meanwhile, their upperbody clothes were either skin tight or left slightly open to reveal some naked flesh.

Karin and Sonya finally became Rudy and Andre's choices. The two girls, who'd been sitting and quietly chatting, immediately got up. The other three girls awkwardly did the same a few moments later. We couldn't imagine how the girls who weren't chosen must be feeling. We didn't know whether they were disappointed or offended.

'Hey, don't be sentimental! They're used to it. This is a matter of buying and selling,' said Andre.

Mammy Tety immediately opened a drawer and took out an order book. The transaction of Rp350,000 (US$35) for three hours, had to be paid in cash upfront. After finishing the payment process, she instructed Karin and Sonya to start doing their job.

The service model at Number 20 was actually not that different from other love houses in Solo, Surabaya or Bandung. The guests had to pay in cash. The house usually provided a car with a driver who also functioned as a security guard.

Despite the fact that the girls at Number 20 were still young, Karin, Sonya, Indah and their friends looked mature behind their stylish make-up. And even though they had to tempt the guests, they were not in your face as one might expect from a streetwalker.

They could communicate well; it was important that they could mix and communicate with guests, who were mostly from high-class backgrounds and were well educated.

Indeed, the girls had already become involved in some hot discussion. They were jovial, laughing as if they had nothing much to worry about. Of course they appeared intimate with the guests, intimacy being one of the most important traits a girl who depends on a man's selection for her livelihood must learn.

In fact, the girls were recruited from villages. Sonya, for instance, came from a village in Cirebon, Java. She'd joined her friends who were already involved in the trade. Even Karin, from Indramayu, admitted that she had once worked in a massage parlour in Kebayoran Lama, South Jakarta.

Those girls who could work at Number 20 were the chosen few. The criterion was not only their age but also their appearance. Most of them were a 160 centimetres tall and good looking. Just as important, they were refined and sufficiently well groomed so that they could appear more interesting and communicate more fluently with the guests.

Working at the house was, according to Besty, more enjoyable than working in a massage parlour. She said that everything was much easier at Number 20. For example, the house cut wasn't that big. Of the total Rp350,000 (US$35) for each job, she would get at least Rp200,000 (US$20).

Karin and Sonya had joined us in the car, and the Terrano car we were driving was moving towards the Cibubur area of Bogor.

It was here that Rudy owned a house, where he lived with two servants. On the way to his house, Karin and Sonya talked about the life they had been leading for the last three years. They were talking more freely now because they weren't afraid of being watched by Mammy Tety. In line with Besty's admission, Karin felt that she preferred working at Number 20 (Karin had previously worked in a massage parlour).

Even though she'd worked as a masseuse, at night she often went out with her female friends to the discotheques. Some of her friends became call girls in the entertainment places in the Mangga Besar district. It was these friends that got Karin interested in the sex business. Money was the ultimate factor in her becoming involved in such a profession.

However, she didn't want to be too obvious like those working in some parlours in Jakarta. Karin's friends took her to Mamma Tety at Number 20. Since that moment she had changed her profession, now being a call girl.

Her previous profession as a masseuse meant Karin was accustomed to dealing with male guests everyday. Before working at the house she had always refused an invitation to have a 'tempra', a term meaning a bed date, but now, like it or not, she had to be ready to do it.

Her income since she started at Number 20 was certainly increasing. When she worked in the massage parlour, at the most she served only two or three guests a day. The amount of the tips she received every day rarely exceeded Rp100,000 (US$10). Remember this was to be expected because the massage she did for the guests was a real massage! There was no extras involved.

At the house she could have two customers a day and she didn't need to work all week. Actually, the advantage of working at Number 20 was not the house fee she got but the excellent tips she received from the guests. The big money she earned was when she conducted her business away from Number 20, either in a private house, an apartment or in a hotel room.

'The money can be three times more than my previous income. No one says no to more cash, do they?' said Karin.

Most of the guests who had a date with Karin were now her loyal customers. Therefore, she knew could certainly expect a decent tip from her regulars. At the most, she worked five days a week and the money she earned was not less than Rp3 million (US$300) per week, an incredibly high income for the average uneducated village girl in Indonesia.

Meanwhile, Sonya had a different story to tell. Formerly, she'd been roaming her hometown working as a middle-tier call girl. Fulfilling orders from hotels or private requests became her daily job. She admitted she knew someone who regularly set her up with dates.

'The contact person happened to be a hotelier. So it was easier to get an order,' she said.

Unfortunately, the impact of the monetary crisis in her home town made living costs increase, meaning it was time for her to move to Jakarta for better opportunities.

Her friends from the same profession had been very helpful to her when she started in Jakarta, so she found it quite easy to enter the jungle of Jakarta's nightlife. She said that two of her closest friends had been working as call girls in Jakarta. Sonya had joined up with them and between them, their pimp lined up two or three jobs a week, with earnings of up to Rp1 million (US$100) per job.

She moved to Number 20 because she felt that there was a more constant flow of work and also that there was potential to earn good money in tips.

'If I'm lucky, I can get Rp1 or 2 million [US$100 or 200] per date now,' she said.

When we reached his house, Rudy made us all welcome, plying us with food and alcohol. Karin and Sonya's friendliness and intimacy made Rudy change his mind. He called Mammy Tety. The short-time booking was now changed to a long-time or overnight booking by paying an additional amount of Rp1 million (US$100) per person. Their status as members made it easy for Rudy and Andre to do this over the phone.

For Rudy and Andre this evening was not just their second or third time taking girls out from Number 20, it was actually about their seventh time. Normally, the house could expect ten bookings a day. On busy days, especially at the weekends, it could be as high as twenty a day.

This meant the house could earn about Rp50 million (US$5000) per month. Of course this was an illegal business, but what could be done about it? Monied men looking for sex will offer what it takes and with enough money, especially in a country as poor as Indonesia, anything is attainable.

Desperate Housewives

Rich, lonely women, determined to have fun, party the night away in clubs, discotheques, cafés and private houses. In their quest for companionship they seek out Charlie, who promises them all an earthly paradise.

It was late evening in Jakarta. A heavy downpour had done its best to wash away the sins of the city. But, in a luxury house in an affluent suburb, four women and a tall white man were laughing gleefully. Garage music played on the stereo. The clock on the wall ticked loudly, reminding people of the lateness of the hour.

On a glass table was a selection of Cognac and whisky, including Hennessy and Chivas. Alongside were some colourful pills wrapped in thin, transparent plastic packaging. There were three glasses of iced drinks. Next to the whisky bottle was a small black tray.

Laughter and uninhibited dancing coloured the night until early in the morning, and still the beautiful girls didn't seem to tire. The coolness of the air-conditioned room was sending some others to sleep; I could only smile grimly as I joined in the dancing, trying desperately to stay awake.

It was such a crazy night. I had never expected that Dewita's invitation would lead to an all-night party. A former model and singer from the late

80s, Dewita was in her thirties and wealthy.

It all began when I met Putri, a twenty-eight-year-old model whose sisters had been famous celebrities. She'd invited me to attend an event held in a top café, Manna Lounge, at Taman Ria Senayan.

I had known Putri for quite a long time. She was a public figure, easily recognized thanks to her starring roles in various TV productions. Putri always tried to find time to visit some of the elite entertainment places. Her favourite places were the fashionable cafés in South and Central Jakarta.

The party at Manna Lounge Café was a grandiose affair at which Putri introduced me to three friends of hers and also to a tall white man, who had a shaved head and a thin moustache. Richard worked as a DJ.

The three girls were Dewita, Leni and Mary. Leni was about twenty-seven years old with short hair and a size-twelve figure. Leni, who liked wearing miniskirts, was the daughter of a former key official, who now runs his own restaurant business in the Kemang area of South Jakarta.

Mary was a widow with a child. She was in her mid-thirties and ran her own business buying and selling antiques. She had two big outlets in the Ciputat district and one more outlet in Surabaya Street. Her deceased husband had left her a large inheritance, one that was more than enough to fulfil her daily needs for many years to come.

Dewita, as I've already mentioned, was formerly a singer and a model, and was married to a rich man. It was said that her husband was a Chinese businessman who had companies everywhere. Unfortunately, Dewita was only his second wife. She occupied a big house in the Kemang district and a luxury apartment in Kuningan.

Her status as a second wife meant that she ran her life like that of a single woman. So, it wasn't surprising that Dewita spent more time with her close friends than with her husband.

In her own mind, it was acceptable for her to spend hours in cafés, pubs and nightclubs. After all, she had to kill the boredom somehow. In one night she and her friends would go to three or four different places.

Although Dewita was financially comfortable, her time alone meant that she wasn't truly happy. In her loneliness, life felt very uncertain. Her nights out with her friends were a way of deflecting this feeling.

She felt doubly empty because she hadn't got a baby yet. She had been a wife in a wealthy environment for more than five years, yet she had nothing. Financially, Dewita was never lacking. She lived in luxury. On the face of it Dewita had everything she needed. Just not true happiness.

Even though the restaurants that Leni ran were not really busy every day, the profit she made was more than enough to live in luxury. She had a big house, a BMW 5 Series, expensive jewellery and so forth.

Meanwhile, Mary, who was a widow, had more than enough wealth. Her antiques business had given her ever-increasing profits. And Putri, even though she was not as famous as some high-end celebrities, had a Western husband who fulfilled all of her daily needs. Although he rarely lived in Jakarta, every month he sent Putri thousands of dollars.

Well, that's how the girls were. Materially speaking, they were wealthy. Everything was available and all of their daily needs were fulfilled. However, there was something deprived from them, an innate necessity: affection.

Dewita was always lonely because she could only be with her husband two or three times a month. Not to mention her frustration of not being able to have a child, which she had been hoping for such a long time.

Leni was in a similar predicament. Rarely did she get a man's true love. Or how about Mary, who lived in luxury but had an empty soul because she didn't know where to direct her life. Or Putri, who had little self-confidence because she hadn't reached the peak of her career, not to mention her husband who was rarely at her side.

It was because the girls were basically in the same boat that they felt a close affinity with each other. They became like a small club of rich women who were lonely without their husbands. The desperate housewives. So it was that they found themselves roaming the cafés, pubs and discotheques, and eventually taking solace in recreational drugs.

With money, these girls could easily get any men they liked. But why bother when such happiness only lasts a very short time and is based only on lust? They actually wanted more than that—to be loved and pampered by the men they loved.

As arranged, we met at Dewita's apartment in Kuningan at seven. The apartment was on the twelfth floor but we met up in the lobby where Dewita had been standing by, waiting for us.

After everyone had gathered in the lobby, we went upstairs. Dewita's apartment was number 1216. The flat was small, but luxurious. There was a living room with a brown sofa, a television, and a small table in each corner on which sat a vase containing fresh flowers.

Its biggest room was the bedroom with its large bed and a sky blue bed sheet. It was this room that had become Dewita's palace.

Dewita, Leni, Mary and Putri looked comfortable in each other's company. While lighting a cigarette, Dewita invited me to pour myself a drink. On the shelf was a row of bottles, which were arranged neatly in order.

As Leni mixed a glass of Chivas Regal and ginger ale, Dewita ordered dinner over the telephone. At the same time, Mary was busy touching up her make-up.

Less than half an hour later, like a family, we enjoyed dinner together. There was chicken, steak and fresh salad. We enjoyed the food and we chatted amiably, while RnB music filled the room.

We finished our dinner and continued our relaxed chatter, intimate jokes frequently colouring the night air. The girls looked fresh and beautiful in their stylish attire, classy jewellery and make-up. They looked doubly enchanting because the atmosphere was lighter now, the girls happier and less lonely.

At about nine, the evening's entertainment took a new twist. On the dining table was a small black tray holding some white powder with a rolled up 100-dollar note.

'It's time for Charlie,' squealed Dewita.

She took the tray and heated it briefly in the microwave. She then cut the powder into neat lines on the tray. One by one, they used the 100-dollar bill to snort the cocaine, rubbing any leftovers on their gums.

Their faces looked fresher. The music was changed to a more upbeat trance and garage rhythm. The girls now began to dance.

It wasn't until eleven that we left the apartment. The first place we visited was the JC Club at LM hotel in Senayan. Here we continued dancing and drinking. Several of the girls' friends dropped by and joined in with us.

At one o'clock in the morning we left JC Club and went to RT, a bar-cum-discotheque in the Gatot Subroto district. In the car, the girls shared an ecstasy pill between them. Dewita took half of it and Leni, Mary, and Putri got one sixth each. One of them said that the pill was obtained from the Netherlands.

'Hey, you know, this is an original product. Don't overdose,' joked Dewita.

As soon as we arrived at RT, the girls were quickly absorbed in the rhythm of trance and garage music, which was pounding out from the speakers. They seemed very alert, as their bodies followed the rhythm of the music. Beads of sweat appeared on their faces.

It was in RT that they met Richard, the DJ from London, who had previously put on some very good performances at some of the fashionable cafés in Jakarta and Bali.

At three thirty, RT was closing so they decided to continue the night's roadshow at the SD discotheque in the city area. At the entrance to SD, Dewita again shared a party pill with her friends.

'Hey, I'm about to drop. Give me my share, will you?' whispered Leni, who then immediately lost herself in the heaving dance floor.

The house music, which dominated at SD, got them even more

worked up. I could only shake my head, wondering what they could get out of such a wild experience. The girls certainly looked happy, they were full of zest with wide grins.

When I looked at my watch, I realised that it was nearly eight in the morning. We left soon after and returned to Dewita's place. Richard joined us.

Back at Dewita's apartment, the party was still very much alive. Dewita took out the black tray once more. She also placed three more ecstasy pills on the table and Richard divided them into several small pieces. I shook my head when Richard offered me a small piece.

'Sorry, I'm not used to taking it. I'll just have a drink, thanks,' I said, refusing as politely as I could.

The party continued as they snorted Charlie and popped pills. It seemed to me that the pills were being bandied about like sweets.

The temperature was increasing as morning gradually became midday. It was already eleven when Richard, a handsome guy, became the girls' main target. I don't know who started it but all of a sudden Dewita and Leni began kissing him passionately. I knew nothing of what happened next as by now I had finally succumbed to my sleepiness.

When I woke up at four that afternoon I found Leni and Dewita laying on one bed in the main bedroom and Mary and Putri in another bedroom. There were clothes strewn all over the flat but there was no sign of Richard! I could only imagine what had taken place but I'm sure that whatever it was, these ladies had successfully escaped their problems for another night at least.

'Melrose Place' Jakarta-style

Glittery and full of promise from the outside, this downtown apartment block is really a den of iniquity. Within its corridors of power, passion and pills, life plays out like a bad American soap opera where the characters ultimately have nowhere to go but down.

My friend and I hadn't actually intended to go to Edelweiss apartment block at Mangga Dua in metropolitan Jakarta.

Levy, a model whose face could be seen in the entertainment magazines and tabloids, had invited us to her place for dinner.

'I'll introduce you to some of my friends. They're beautiful,' she'd said.

Levy got on with nearly everybody. As a newcomer to the world of modelling, the twenty-year-old from Semarang in Java was friendly and confident. She was sociable and easy to talk to but I didn't yet know whether she was only being friendly because we were journalists or if she was like this with everybody. But of course we couldn't refuse a dinner invitation from a beautiful woman like Levy.

Edelweiss was situated in MGS street in the residential and trade area of Mangga Dua. The apartment building looked luxurious enough with a high fence and a magnificent gate. The nickname 'Mini Melrose

Place' seemed to be fairly appropriate. Two security guards guarded the entrance door.

On entering the front yard, we saw around twenty parked cars, from BMWs to SUVs. We walked up to the entrance. In the building's lobby there was a notice board on which some rules and regulations were posted. One of these said that guests weren't allowed to visit a resident in the apartment after midnight.

'Hey, nobody worries about the rule. Ignore it,' said Levy who came down to fetch us after we contacted her via the intercom.

Walking down a corridor, we saw a row of numbered, light blue doors. Next to the doors, along the stark white corridor, were groups of chairs and tables neatly arranged. At that time, it was already eight in the evening. Several couples were talking intimately at the tables. Some of the women wore only shorts and T-shirts.

Before reaching a flight of stairs, we passed a small garden and an aquarium set into the wall. Not far from the aquarium was a canteen, where some men were sitting at the tables.

'Let's go to the fifth floor,' suggested Levy.

There was no lift. We took the stairs, which I noted were white porcelain, to the fifth floor. On passing the second, third and fourth floors we sneaked a look into their corridors—more of the same blue doors.

'My room's at the end,' said Levy, upon reaching the fifth floor.

We arrived at Number 408. To the right of the door, there was a second, decorative door made of iron. Through gaps in this iron door we took a peek at the view behind it. We could see the settlements beyond the apartment complex. Closer in there were tables, chairs and plants—this must have been a garden terrace.

Levy invited us in. The chill from the air conditioning hit us as we passed through the door. Fluorescent lamps shone brightly, allowing us to see that the room was full of furniture and clothes. It seemed pretty small to justify the rent of Rp2 million (US$200).

The flat was open plan, with a sofa bed in the main room and a bathroom located near the entrance door. The most interesting articles were Levy's photos, hanging on the white walls. All of them depicted Levy in sexy poses, in fact a couple of them showed her almost naked.

Some of these pictures had been published in magazines, other in the tabloids. Her bathroom proudly displayed more large framed photos. We were gazing at the prints when Levy broke the silence.

'Let me change my clothes first, OK?' she said.

Levy, whom I should add was tall and had shoulder-length wavy hair, opened her wardrobe. My God! She must have had hundreds of clothes stashed away.

She selected a thin, virtually transparent dress and took it with her into the shower area. The sound of cascading water drifted over from the bathroom.

We decided to sit down on the bed and turned on the 29-inch TV. The Cinemax channel was playing although I wasn't really paying any attention to it as I looked round the room.

On the TV console there was a complete multimedia set-up: VCD and LD players and a hi-fi. I could see four speakers: two near the television, and two fixed to the wall on brackets in the right and left corners of the room. Stacks of VCDs and LDs were arranged in order next to the television. We flipped through the VCDs. Wow! Some of the covers depicted sex scenes ... blue films!

The door of the bathroom opened and Levy appeared with her hair wrapped in a towel. Her thin dress barely disguised her slim and sexy body. Her panties could be clearly seen, as could her pert breasts pressing against the material of her dress. She didn't appear to be embarrassed even though there were two men in front of her.

'Let me call in Vivi and Anita,' said Levy while pressing the phone numbers 419 and 212.

It seemed that she wanted to invite some of her friends.

Levy then dropped herself onto the mattress. This was distracting! While lighting her favorite cigarette, a Dunhill Light, Levy changed the

TV channel.

'Why don't we sing karaoke? It's exciting,' she offered, getting up from her seat.

She then took a CD from her collection of the most popular national songs. While she was singing Alda's 'Aku Tak Biasa', Vivi and Anita came into the room. The two girls joined us on the bed. Vivi was wearing shorts and a white T-shirt, while Anita was covering her sensual body with a full-length blue dress. The three girls took turns to sing their favourite songs. Anita was singing beautifully and her voice was sweet as she sang Desy Ratnasary's 'Tenda Biru'. After singing five or six numbers, they finished the karaoke with a closing song of Agnes Monica's, 'Pernikahan Dini'.

It was nine fifteen. We inhaled the sweet fragrance of the girls as we listened to their stories. Their talk was focused on their problems with men.

Men. The word became a focal point for Levy, Vivi and Anita whenever they told a new story. Levy, who came from Semarang in Java, told us about her life. She came to Jakarta because her parents were forcing her to marry a man she didn't like, and she already had a lover. Finally, she fled her house together with her boyfriend. She was just seventeen years old.

For six months in Jakarta, Levy and her lover, Agus, lived together in a rented house just like husband and wife. Levy became pregnant but, because they quarrelled frequently, she fled again and had an abortion. In the end, she met a 'pappy' or pimp who employed her as a 'night girl'.

'I would accompany guests for karaoke or a dance,' she said.

That was the starting point for Levy to gradually change her life. Her sexy body and beautiful face led her to the modelling world.

In fact, Vivi, who was just twenty-one years old, and Anita, who was twenty-three years old, had the same profession as Levy. Both of them worked as night girls. Besides accompanying the guests for karaoke, Anita, who had a good voice, was also a successful singer in pubs. She said that she could have cut her first *dangdut* album when she was eighteen if only she'd accepted the invitation to sleep with the producer first.

Meanwhile, Vivi, who came from Jakarta, said that every day she waited to be invited by the bosses to attend a dance or to just accompany people for dinner.

From our chat we understood they were night girls. In Jakarta parlance that does not imply they are necessarily commercial sex workers or prostitutes. Levy, Vivian and Anita spent their nights in karaoke bars, casinos and discotheques, while their days were spent asleep, chatting to neighbours or watching TV. But this didn't mean that they refused sex jobs. They were, after all, girls for hire. However, selling sex was not their main priority when on the job.

The men who became Levy and Anita's 'husbands' could certainly be categorised as rich. Levy's 'husband' was not of Chinese descent, but was a foreign citizen. He was popular enough because he managed a high-class production company. Meanwhile, Anita's 'husband' had an electronic equipment shop in the Mangga Dua area.

On Saturday evenings Edelweiss apartment block was bustling. Dozens of couples occupied the tables in front of the rooms. From the front yard, we could see the garden terraces on every floor, full of men and women who were mingling, joking and laughing. Once in a while, we could hear the sound of tinkling glasses and indulgent sighs from the second floor.

In front of Room 212, we saw Anita sitting on a white man's lap. On seeing us arrive, Anita quickly invited us to drop by for a second. She introduced us to her lover, Dick, the owner of the electronics shop. We were invited to enter Anita's room.

The interior of Anita's room looked exactly the same as that of Levy's. But Anita's room looked larger because she had less furniture in it. There was a 29-inch television, LD player, VCD player, VCR player etc. On the TV console we saw two bongs, which were used to smoke marijuana.

'Do you want to watch a blue film? Don't worry about my husband. He's all right,' said Anita while looking at Dick, who seemed a little embarrassed, although he was smiling.

Anita and Dick seemed familiar with the film. They were relaxed, sitting on the sofa hugging each other. The sound of the TV was very loud, quite why I wasn't sure.

'Watching this kind of film here is a daily thing. Just listen. Those in the room next to this one are probably watching a similar film,' said Anita.

True enough the rooms were not soundproof. Now that I listened closer, I could hear loud sighs from the adjacent flat.

Anita got up from the bed and took down the bongs from the console. From the drawer of her dressing table, Anita took out a small plastic package containing some shiny silver grains of *shabu-shabu*—a type of marijuana—some pieces of thin tin foil that had been moulded to form a bowl with tiny slits in it, and a small primer made from a perfume bottle with a wick in it. Anita took a long hit on the bong, inhaling the smoke from the *shabu-shabu* before Dick followed suit. Every so often, they looked up at the porno film on the TV screen.

Feeling a little uneasy, we said goodbye and left for Levy's room. Both of them accompanied us to the door.

'I'll follow you later. You know, I'm in the mood for sex,' she said candidly.

They immediately closed the door. We went up to the fifth floor.

When we arrived on the fifth floor, we met Vivi, who was giving some money to an office boy. She asked us to drop by, so we entered her room: Number 419. Vivi's room was in the middle of the corridor. To reach it, we passed at least four or five other rooms. In front of Room 215, we met some young couples who were chatting with a woman.

'That's Ayu. She usually works at JM,' said Vivi, trying to explain.

According to Vivi, Ayu frequently held *shabu-shabu* parties together with her friends in her room. The young men provided the goods, while Ayu prepared the room as a venue for the parties.

Before entering Vivi's room, we heard house music playing loudly from a nearby room whose door was closed.

'It's probably Angel tripping with her new man,' Vivi explained.

Vivi's room was open. We were startled to find a bare-chested man, wearing only a pair of shorts, lying on her bed watching a threesome scene play out on a porno film!

'Sorry, I forgot to tell you about him,' said Vivi.

Vivi introduced us to Jo, who hurriedly wore his T-shirt, said goodbye and disappeared downstairs.

Jo, it transpired, lived in the same apartment block as Vivi. He lived on the first floor and worked in a photo studio. His hobbies were gambling and doing drugs.

'I just needed it. Well, that's why I called Jo to come up,' said Vivi.

Oh my God! Vivi hadn't called Jo up for a chat. When Vivi bumped into us, she'd just finished making love to Jo.

On Vivi's dressing table, we found a used mobile phone top-up card. On the card there was still some leftover white powder. Near the used phone card was a short straw that was usually used to drink bottled tea.

'It was Jo who brought it here. I just had a little,' said Vivi.

She then proceeded to finish off the rest of the powder as she lay on the bed. After she'd finished she went to the bathroom.

'I'll take a bath first because I have a date at eleven,' she called over her shoulder.

While Vivi was taking a bath, we were observing her room. There was a big trophy, which was displayed next to the TV. It was an award she received for her achievements in modelling.

On the walls of Vivi's room were some oversized photos taken at ZT, a famous studio. In a glass wardrobe, we could see several porno

VCDs. It was odd that some covers of the VCDs had been changed with the covers showing Vivi in a naked pose.

'Aren't they good? I made them,' said Vivi, who had just come out from the bathroom.

She then took a black gown from her wardrobe but didn't actually put it on. Only wearing a towel, bra and panties she sat indifferently on the chair in front of the mirror. We watched TV with her, feeling a little awkward.

Vivi was now rubbing her sexy body with body lotion. Her oval face and prominent chin was made-up before she applied some thin powder. Her beautiful lips were embellished with maroon lipstick. She wore high-heeled shoes and held a small handbag. The fragrance of her perfume was carried around the room by the fans in the air-conditioning unit.

At eleven thirty, Vivi's mobile phone rang.

'I must go now. Let's go to Levy's room,' suggested Vivi.

The three of us walked up to the fifth floor. We heard some people arguing and, as we turned a corner, we could see Levy quarrelling with another woman. Next to the other woman stood a handsome man with a thin moustache. It seemed that Levy was quarreling with the girl named Mona because Levy had slept with Mona's 'husband'. Other residents who were sitting on their chairs were ignoring what was going on.

Mona was accusing Levy of shamelessly snatching away her man. Levy argued that she didn't ask Mona's husband to sleep with her, that it was the other way around. She claimed it was Mona's husband, Jeffery, who first seduced Levy and invited her to sleep with him.

The three of us were waiting for the argument to blow over. Mona and Jeffery then slammed the door very loudly. Levy was startled when she saw us arriving.

'Sorry, I had a little problem,' she said.

Levy invited us into her room. She didn't turn on the main light;

instead she chose to turn on fairy lights wrapped around some decorative roses on top of the refrigerator. She then played Mariah Carey's 'I Still Believe'.

Unlike the day before, Levy looked gloomy. Without being asked, Levy told us about her problem. Her boyfriend hadn't called her for two weeks. He'd promised to pick her up and go for a walk, but hadn't kept his promise. And her monthly allowance, which usually hit Rp10 million (US$1000), hadn't arrived.

She let her disappointment pour out by inviting Mona's 'husband' to sleep with her. During six months as a secret woman, she was very faithful, which meant that her status as a night girl was only limited to accompanying guests to dinner or sitting on a sofa during a karaoke session. Even that was limited to once or twice a week. Of late, Levy always refused any kind of sex transaction whereas in times past she had been up for anything.

Therefore, her fidelity disappeared when her lover didn't appear to care about her as usual. Levy tempted and seduced her neighbour's 'husband', which was the starting point of her quarrel with Mona.

Mona's 'husband', Jeffery, was actually a GM, or a procurer, who supplied high-class girls as entertainment. The day before, Jeffery had sent three girls to accompany two successful businessmen to a karaoke session with them at TA hotel.

It was now one in the morning. Levy was only wearing hot pants with a tight black T-shirt. Her wavy hair was tied upward with a black scarf.

She stood up and opened a drawer of her dressing table and took out a bong. Thick dirty white smoke was soon billowing in Levy's room. After inhaling at least four or five times, Levy invited us to join her and sit on the chairs outside.

It was already late at night, but there were still some men and women, around six altogether, sitting and talking. In the garden terrace, couples were busy playing cards. We were sitting and smoking. From this vantage point, we could freely observe all the residents of the apartment block.

While listening to Levy's never-ending story, we kept an eye on the corridor. From the stairs on the fourth floor appeared a man and woman walking side by side, entering Room 412.

'She's changed her spouse again,' said Levy.

It seemed that the woman who had just arrived with the man was called Susi. She was twenty-four years old and worked in an insurance company. However, away from her desk she worked as a night girl.

'She has a lot of men. Today she is with that man, tomorrow she'll be with somebody else,' explained Levy.

At around one forty-five Levy said that she wanted to go to DS discotheque in the city.

'I'm tripping while earning some pennies. Who knows, maybe I'll get a bigger one,' she said honestly.

We said our goodbyes. The night had gone on long enough. On the way home, we couldn't understand this metropolitan way of life that was getting crazier and crazier. Was this the same as the lifestyle in the West? A lifestyle à la *Melrose Place*—free sex, spouse swapping and drug use—could be clearly seen at Edelweiss.

Despite being raided several times by the police, Edelweiss was still full of people, both residents and guests. All the rooms were fully occupied. It seemed that its location, which was near the city centre yet reasonably well hidden, and the freedom extended to its residents, made for a near permanent sell-out.

It was an apartment block alive with stories about the lives of the night women with their free and hedonistic lifestyles. From the outside the building looked glittery and full of promise, but this was a mirage, for the place was dark and drowning in the illusion of high-flying lifestyle fuelled by sex and drugs.

Orgies to Order

Orgies are a common theme of blue movies from the West but could the real thing actually exist in Jakarta? It seems it could.

I wouldn't have dropped by the Zanzibar café in Kebayoran Baru, South Jakarta, had it not been raining heavily from midday right through to the early evening. The long tailbacks on the busy streets forced me to stop and wait it out with a coffee and some warm garlic bread.

And I would surely have left Zanzibar by eight o'clock if Antoni, a twenty-nine-year-old friend of mine, hadn't suddenly appeared in front of my table. Antoni was a good friend I'd known for about two years. A single guy, he spent much of his time in a fashionable café called AT in the Surdiman district, where he worked as an operations manager. He had frequently accompanied me on various trips to the local cafés and discotheques.

It was Antoni who often supplied me with information about the nightlife in and around Jakarta. It was understandable that he knew so much because the scope of his job introduced him to people from many different walks of life, all of whom were very fond of wandering around the city at night.

Our plan to spend only one or two hours in the café changed somewhat as we drank and talked into the night. I think we must have spent at least four hours in there, starting on coffee and then moving onto

Black Russians. I downed three glasses, while Antoni got through more than three shots of Jack Daniel's on the rocks.

From the tug-of-war between cafés and restaurants to the latest love scandals of local actresses, we certainly covered some ground as we chatted about the wild and wonderful nightlife scene in Jakarta. We also talked about 'order girls'—the call girls who are now leaving their dens and operating in the more up-market cafés, and also about the brand new 'menus' being offered by a number of new entertainment places.

Our discussion finally touched on a place that we had only visited two or three times together. This place was known as a 'taking-in' house and housed over fifty girls ready to provide on-the-spot sex services, perhaps disguised as massage.

The idea of dropping by there was suddenly mooted by Antoni. He said that he hadn't visited Susi, who was slim and had long hair, bright skin and an oval face, for a long time. He also told me how friendly Linda was and how skillful she was at entertaining guests in her playful style.

'Well, you know, I've heard there are new girls. And there's a new service which is supposed to be wild,' said Antoni, while laughing loudly.

Our car sped on, splashing through large puddles of water on the sodden streets. From Zanzibar café we crossed the big intersection that demarcates the border of South and Central Jakarta. After that we swung left, passing the market in the Mayestik district, onto AP Street, a main thoroughfare in South Jakarta.

Less than two hundred metres later, the traffic lights turned red. We stopped in the left lane, then turned left onto CP Street when the lights changed. This street was famous for its massage parlours. No less than five large establishments were based here, with big, fancy nameplates and tariffs to match.

After we passed PH massage parlour, a place famous for its beautiful girls, we finally arrived at the taking-in house.

It wasn't what you might imagine, being situated among a row of shops. A large nameplate with the letters, BO, identified the house. We stopped our car in front of the building. About five cars were parked in the frontyard. Next to BO was a beauty parlour called RT Salon Hair and Beauty. To the other side of the salon was what we looked to be an office building.

The floor of BO was finished in white porcelain tiles. On the ground floor was a single receptionist who was busy reading a magazine. The only furnishings were a set of chairs and a table.

We were then invited to go upstairs. On the first floor was a long black sofa. Two girls welcomed us and immediately invited us to take a seat for a while.

The living room, or perhaps more precisely the waiting room, was not that big. There were two short sofas and one long sofa next to a black glass table. Next to that was a reception desk where two girls were waiting.

Well, we didn't really need to bother ourselves with the niceties because Antoni had already chosen some girls before we got there. As returning guests we thought we wouldn't need to have a look at the photo albums of girls at BO, but as it was rumoured there were new girls, we decided to look anyway.

'This is Maya. She's been here just one month, a pretty girl from Bandung. While this one, who has lovely skin, is Ria. She is still only twenty-two,' said the receptionist who had short hair and tanned skin.

For several minutes we looked through the album. There weren't actually that many new girls, seven or eight at the most. Meanwhile, two of the faces that we recognized, Linda and Susi, still featured in the album.

For places not using the fishbowl method of selection, a photo album could be useful as a guide for a first-time visitor. Even though the actual girl usually turned out to be different to her photograph at least a guest could have a rough idea of the girl might look like.

Antoni seemed to be less taken by the new girls and stuck to Susi. I gambled on Maya. Well, who could tell from a photo? Maya looked sexier than Susi!

'Do you want to do it here directly or take her out? If you want to take her out, the price will be a bit higher,' explained the receptionist.

From the beginning, we had agreed to do everything in house. We told the receptionist that we would do a direct transaction.

Instead of spending extra time looking for a hotel, we chose the faster dine-in service. Besides, the incessant drizzle made us weary of going out on the streets again.

'If there's a kinky offer, just take it. I heard the girls here can be persuaded to have orgies,' whispered Antoni, while gently hitting my shoulder.

The receptionist opened the door and invited us in. We were asked to choose one of the rooms facing us. There were about ten rooms set in two rows, facing each other. So, there were about twenty rooms that BO had provided.

I chose the room at the end of the row, while Antoni chose the room in the middle. The rooms were numbered and the doors were covered with green curtains. The rooms were brightly lit, while the air conditioning made the rooms cool and comfortable. To complete the relaxing atmosphere was softly playing music.

It was five past eight in the evening when Maya knocked at the door. She wasn't much different from what I'd seen in the photo album. In fact she was even more beautiful in the flesh. She was about 168 centimetres tall, had brown skin and shoulder-length straight hair. A true beauty.

Maya was wearing a black jacket, but underneath this was a sleeveless, striped blue shirt with a matching miniskirt. To cover her legs, she was wearing soft brown stocking with high-heeled shoes.

Maya introduced herself, speaking in a clear Sundanese dialect. She tried to make me feel as comfortable as possible with her friendly small talk. She ran her fingers through her hair as she spoke, a subtle and erotic touch that was probably subconscious.

The scene with Maya and I was like any other potential love transaction across Jakarta between a guest and his chosen girl. Only now Maya moved the goalposts somewhat when she suddenly offered something a little new.

'If you are served by one girl only, it's normal, isn't it? You're accustomed to doing it, aren't you? But how about with two or three girls at the same time? If it's OK, I'll call them right now,' said Maya matter-of-factly.

This was the offer that Antoni had told me about before we came in. It seemed that what Antoni had called a kinky offer was actually a euphemism for orgy sex.

Being naturally curious, I agreed to Maya's offer! In less than ten minutes Maya came back with another girl. She introduced her to me as Linda. I remembered that Linda was one of Antoni's favourite girls.

I had never expected to be offered orgy sex at BO. Although I'd been roaming around night entertainment joints that were categorized as triple-X in Jakarta for quite a long time, I still felt clumsy. My heart was beating faster and faster as the seconds ticked by.

My mind immediately recalled the hot scenes shown in blue films when a man was having sex with two, three or even four women at the same time. Was it this that was being offered to me now?

It was. With lights set low, and an atmosphere less intimidating than the 'porno version', the orgy was acted out for real.

Such a sex service was a relatively new phenomenon. BO, with its orgy girls certainly looked after its guests. It didn't matter if a guest had to spend Rp350,000 (US$35) excluding tips for the girls, plus Rp95,000 (US$10) for the hire of the room.

Again, this is Jakarta. I don't know of anywhere else in Indonesia where one can be offered such a variety of entertainment venues. Jakarta is Jakarta, its face reflecting all the colours of metropolitan life.

On the way home Antoni and I talked endlessly about the orgy service given by the girls at BO. In my heart, I kept on questioning myself—would Jakarta be associated from now on with a lipstick, free love and cash lifestyle?

Gambling on Sex

Compared to Jakarta's sex workers, whose whole lives are a gamble, the city's high-rollers have it easy. In illegal casinos throughout Jakarta, big-time gamblers play the tables and play the women who work there.

Illegal doesn't necessarily mean something cannot be found. In Jakarta, the business of gambling can never be extinguished. Even though officials frequently raid them, gambling dens continue to exist.

There were at least four big gambling centres in early 2002, operating round the clock. The first was in Ancol, the second in Kelapa Gading, while the third and fourth were located in the Kota and Mangga Dua areas respectively.

An interesting thing about gambling venues is their implicit association with beautiful women and sex. Either in the context of women as the players or as accessories of the high-rolling gamblers, women as objects of visual and sexual gratification just seem to blend in seamlessly in the shady world of professional gambling. Everyone knows that besides being a city of casinos, Las Vegas has also become a centre of prostitution.

What about Jakarta? The answer is clear: there is no difference. Gambling … women … everything inevitably culminates in a sexual transaction. This vignette of gambling in Jakarta is particularly true of the larger elite gambling arenas.

It was almost three in the morning when I arrived at one of the biggest gambling houses in Jakarta. There was no signage as with a café or club; the building's facade looked like a large warehouse and it was surrounded by a high fence. If the average man on the street glanced at the building he would never imagine it was a gambling arena.

The gamblers called the place MDR. It was easy to find due to its strategic location near to some entertainment and shopping centres— MDR was actually situated not far from a shopping mall in Kelapa Gading.

Of course this wasn't the first time I'd visited MDR. I'd gone several times before to try out the various types of gambling games that seemed to be attracting a lot of visitors, both male and female. There were those who went alone, others who went in groups, even some who brought the whole family!

On entering MDR, the first thing that met the eye was the wide parking lot, which could accommodate more than 200 vehicles. At three in the morning, as I'd expected, MDR's parking lot was full. It was safe enough to leave your vehicle at this illegal gambling den because the carpark was managed by Secure Parking—a well-known company that operates most of the carparks in big cities throughout Indonesia!

When I stepped inside the gambling hall, everybody was still busy with their own game, seemingly oblivious to the time, and the darkness outside. Punters were wildly pressing buttons on slot machines, trying their luck at 'Mickey Mouse', usually known as MM, a popular seven-card gambling game.

MDR was a two-storey building. On the first floor the main game was Mickey Mouse. There were about 150 slot machines, split into three sections: those requiring a 25 token, a 50 token and a 250 token. A 50 denomination token cost Rp5000 (50 US cents). If a punter wanted to play, first of all he had to buy the tokens from a cashier station.

On the second floor were some other machine games such as keno, more popularly known at MDR as UFO. The method of playing it was very simple. Like a lottery, a player picked his number or numbers, pressed the buttons and hoped for some or all of his numbers to be chosen. There were more than 100 machines in use and every night the place was busy.

There were many types of other games offered at MDR. There were four types of wins that every player was waiting for: a Royal Flush, *Goki*, *STR* and *Siki*. With the 50 token, for example, a player who got a Royal Flush could win Rp12 million (US$1200), for *Goki*, a player could get about Rp6 million (US$600), for *STR* about Rp3 million (US$300), and for *Siki* about Rp1 million (US$100). This didn't include the main jackpot prize in the form of a car that could be awarded to a player who successfully got the Royal Flush between nine in the morning and ten at night.

It was these temptations that ensured MDR was permanently full of visitors. The gambling tables created their own stories, and there was usually room for tales of sexual transactions.

Almost forty percent of the punters who played at Kunir were women. Many didn't seem to care what time of the day it was. Twenty-four hours a day, there were women gambling there, the numbers continuously self-replenishing. Some even stayed from one morning to the next.

It was no secret that some of these gambling women were also looking for pick-ups. And not for free. Usually, they would do the 'shopping trip' from one machine to another, trying to find the lucky man who got a Royal Flush, *Goki*, *STR* or *Siki*.

It was also widely known that the 'lucky' men of the gambling tables liked to throw their money around. One way of doing this was to invite any one of the many women who'd made MDR their base for an all-night date; of course for an agreed price. The modus operandi of these women was therefore pretty straightforward.

Even though most of the people who frequented MDR were 'players', they were from different backgrounds and circumstances. The male players, for example, were mostly businessmen, of whom quite a few were of Chinese descent, while most of the females had double status—many worked in karaoke lounges as escorts, while others were call girls.

At the keno machines all players were provided with soft sofas with two machines arranged side by side. The sofas were large enough to seat four people. Here I observed men and women mixing freely on the sofas whilst concentrating intently on the games but also call girls who were basically waiting for an opportunity to snatch their man.

I witnessed the glittering nightlife at Kunir for about a month. It felt like watching human beings struggling with their life destiny. The following I witnessed early one morning at the MM table and I'm sure this was a scene being repeated all over gambling dens in Kunir and elsewhere.

Two call girls, who'd just been to a discotheque, now wanted to try their luck at the MM machines.

While playing, they stole a glance around, looking at the men who were busy counting the cards on the screens of the slot machines. Shamelessly, the two girls, one of whom was called Susan, approached a man who was enjoying a winning streak.

'Win the bet, honey? We better celebrate! Want us to accompany you?' she said temptingly.

The short-haired man wearing casual clothes, who'd won at least Rp10 million (US$1000) that night, smiled and quickly responded: 'You want to go now?'

What happened next is easy to imagine. They left Kunir at about three o'clock in the morning. The transaction would probably take place in a hotel room and would last the rest of the night.

Another aspect of MDR was the fact that its hundreds of casino staff were on duty twenty-four hours a day. They were mostly female, beautiful and tempting. Many of the regulars at Kunir were close to the girls. These female front of house staff would chat intimately to male guests who were playing the machines. Whenever the men won, they always gave big tips to the women looking after them.

Girls employed at MDR were very good at taking any opportunity that presented itself for a liaison with a male guest, especially if the girl was pretty and needed the money. It frequently happened that when they changed shift in the mornings, many of the girls had already made an appointment with a guest for a hotel booking away from the casino.

Kunir may have been the biggest gambling arena in Jakarta but HR was better in terms of class, types of games and the special services provided. Located next to a shopping centre in Mangga Dua, HR represented the industry benchmark for illegal gambling arenas in Jakarta.

All kinds of gambling games could be found at HR, ranging from slot machines such as keno, Mickey Mouse and Happy Royal to more traditional casino card-based games such as those found in Las Vegas and Australia.

What set HR apart from the rest was its better range of games, its international standards and its VIP rooms, where escorts were made available for the guests.

I recall one night when a friend of mine, Christian, who was thirty-one years old and ran an electronics factory, invited me to HR to experience the special services offered to VIPs. Christian, who already had a child, frequently spent his evenings and weekends moving from café to café and pub to pub.

That evening, at eleven o'clock, Christian, his assistant and I reached HR. As a wealthy member of the casino, an usher wearing a safari costume immediately met Christian. That evening, Chris, as he was known, had an appointment with some important bosses to play at the VIP casino.

The VIP room was joined to the main casino, but its location was closer to one corner. After passing hundreds of machines in the main room, we finally arrived at the VIP room.

The door to this exclusive room was being watched by several security guards and inside was a round casino table at which sat three middle-aged men who welcomed Chris warmly.

The money that was going down in chips was of course not for the faint-hearted; the bets were topping Rp100 million (US$10,000). This was of no interest to me though, I was far more intrigued by the stunning escorts who served the men during the game!

The escorts were not merely serving, they also treated the men as their lovers for the whole twelve hours the game took to finish. They performed for the men whatever services they were requested to do and they were also ready to move on to a special date with a guest if required.

This they did in return for tips. Whenever one of the players won a big hand, the girls were generously tipped. This happened numerous times over the course of the game. The players frequently teased the girls just for fun before handing them a few hundred thousand rupiah. It was this special service offered at, or under, the gambling table that had become the main attraction for these high rollers.

Even though another casino, '1000', more commonly known as SS, only had a small gambling arena with about 100 machines, it was also well patronised by punters who wanted to taste the gambling buzz and 'earthly desires' all in one place.

Located on the fourth floor of a shopping mall in Hayam Wuruk Street, in the city area, SS was open twenty-four hours a day. It was here that attractive female gamblers could often be found playing the slot machines. Most of them came from other entertainment joints in the city area—they comprised escorts from karaoke bars, strippers and call girls from nearby hotels.

Sitting in SS at about two thirty one morning, I observed how the women playing the slot machines mixed with the male gamblers without a second thought. They would immediately become intimate with the men who were sitting next to them. It was in this fashion that sex deals were usually brokered. The women continued to play the slot machines while trying to spread their charm until they caught the attention of a man.

As well as slot machines, SS also offered baccarat tables presided over by croupiers, a private club, a discotheque and a karaoke. Most karaoke sessions ended with some form of sexual gratification. The escorts at SS, also known as 'singers' or 'madames', were willing to perform a special service such as striptease in the privacy of the karaoke booth for a price. For Rp1 million (US$100) they could be booked for an overnight date.

Competing for the honour of being the casino with the most unusual extra services at one time in Jakarta must have been CPBN. Located in a hotel in Ancol, CPBN thoughtfully offered weary gamblers sauna sex.

At the CPBN VIP sauna, guests could choose their own partners to share a sauna with and they mostly used the sauna as a stopover after they'd finished in the casino. The charge of Rp400,000 (US$40) per hour was nothing for these men who were accustomed to spending millions at the tables.

Gambling and saunas at CPBN seemed to complement each other and the service was frequently used by players who managed to make a huge profit on cards or slot machines.

Jakarta's gambling dens were not only represented by MDR, SS, HR and CPBN. There were similar venues along Gadjah Mada Street, such as Raja Kota, Tahiti and Casanova and along Hayam Wuruk Street. These places were well-known. Every day these casinos were packed with people convinced it was their lucky day.

The portrait of the four casinos offered above seemed to affirm that gambling could barely be separated from women.

When I was trying to leave SS for the last time, a pretty girl wearing a black dress smiled at me warmly. Only one sentence was necessary: 'Good evening, may I join the party?'

In mid-2002 the authorities closed down all the gambling dens in Jakarta without exception. A few defiant ones continued to operate but they too closed down eventually. But this is Jakarta and anything can be found if you look hard enough.

Ladies Night

In a great show of sexual equality, Jakarta's monied ladies throw a wild poolside party where the sex workers are men.

Two handsome men with broad shoulders and athletic bodies were relaxing at VT café in SG mall in Central Jakarta. Seated next to them, three stylish women were chatting away. Placed in front of them, on the chocolate-coloured tablecloth was a selection of snacks and soft drinks.

It was four o'clock in the afternoon and SG mall was very busy as usual. I found myself there, sitting one table away from the party of five, as I had an appointment with a friend. Bram, a twenty-eight-year-old gay man who worked for a modelling agency, wanted to introduce me to some of his latest models, both male and female.

He arrived soon after and ordered an iced cappuccino. Wearing black trousers and a dark blue shirt with a fur bag draped from his shoulder, the well-groomed young man took a seat. This was the second time we'd met. The first time I'd met him was at a party when he'd introduced himself, telling me all about the talents on his company's books.

So it was at the VT café that we met one week later. With his graceful and confident style, Bram showed me the models' photographs one by one. About twenty minutes later however, we were suddenly distracted.

Two of the women from the table directly behind us had very

obviously smiled at Bram. Actually, he'd been periodically looking over at their table, the same one with the two men and the three women that I'd also been observing for the last half an hour or so.

Bram suddenly got up and went over to their table. Amazingly, Bram in fact recognised them. The first woman was Ms Rie and the second Ms Sus. Although their faces suggested they were middle-aged, they looked very sprightly and exciting.

They proved to be quite charming and friendly. It seemed they enjoyed an easy life and it was easy to listen to them chatting away confidently for an hour or so.

Eventually we started to talk about the two men (who had left about thirty minutes earlier). Bram sulkily told the women that he had fallen for one of the two men. Ms Rie said that she had done business with the men several times before and that they'd just promised to put on a performance at a private party in Ms Sus's house.

'They aren't just ordinary guys, they're dancers. We've hired them twice before,' admitted Ms Sus.

I was a little surprised because they were quite bulky men and didn't really look like dancers to me. I didn't doubt the girls though.

Our chat with them drew to a close with them inviting us both to attend their party. By the time we said goodbye I realised I didn't know anything about their background. Bram told me that he knew them both from a socialite group of very rich women. These ladies would meet up and attend social gatherings, parties and often just hang out in the expensive antiques and jewellery shops.

But don't be misled, for they were not dependent on their husbands' money. Most of them ran their own businesses, turning over tens of millions of rupiah a day.

Ms Rie, for example, ran an antiques business and a boutique called LT, selling a collection of imported branded clothes. Meanwhile, Ms Sus had a café-restaurant business in the Surdiman Street area. Both of them were divorced and had become single parents.

Ms Sus's house was situated in an elite complex in Permata Hijau and looked magnificent from the outside. It wasn't difficult to find, as it wasn't far from the main street. A high iron fence surrounded it, in the middle of which was a security post. We arrived at eight o'clock, the guards opening the gate for us as we drove in. Four very expensive cars were already parked in front of the house.

At the front terrace, Ms Sus was talking with some people. I could see five women wearing party clothes and three men dressed in black. Ms Rie was wearing a long, V-shaped black gown, while Ms Sus was wearing a blue knee-length dress.

The guests talked and shared jokes over glasses of chilled wine. The garden, which contained a small pool and some decorative lamps created a very serene setting.

At about nine o'clock, there were already fifteen guests present. Most of them were women. Ms Sus announced that the party was about to begin so all of the guests, Bram and myself included, went inside.

The living room was luxurious. Displayed on its white floor was an impressive black leaf motif. A shiny, black sofa was the main feature in the middle of the room. Under the sofa was spread a red carpet, while a crystal chandelier was shining from above.

A television and some audio-visual equipment were the main contents of the cupboard facing the chairs for the guests. The creamy walls of the room were covered with photos and paintings. One photo was of Ms Sus, in which a man and a young girl wearing Javanese clothes accompanied her.

I thought it was in the living room that the party would be held. In fact, Ms Sus and Ms Rie soon invited us to go to the poolside.

The party continued as the mainly female guests were still heard talking away. They seemed to talk endlessly to each other about anything and everything. The name gossiping gang seemed suitable for them! The sound of their laughter was competing with the music from the living room. It occurred to me that this party was more like a family gathering.

All of the guests who were invited by Ms Sus were her close friends.

The merriment of the private party moved up a notch when Ms Sus introduced three male dancers to the crowd. Everyone applauded as the three men appeared, wearing tight trousers and shiny black shirts.

The three male dancers took up a position directly beside the swimming pool. Meanwhile, the guests jostled for position, trying to find the ideal spot from where they could see the action.

The men began their dance routine, their erotic moves and tempting style garnering differing reactions from the party guests. Some danced to the music while cheering, while others could only open their eyes wide while enjoying their drinks.

The dancers, who were gentle and athletic at the same time, moved their bodies in unison with the disco music. Standing near Ms Sus, I could only smile and laugh when seeing the reactions of the women. Wearing jeans, a T-shirt and a leather jacket, Bram, who indeed liked a partner of the same sex, could not hide his appreciation, as he got more and more absorbed in the music and sensual dancing.

I'd already guessed what might happen next. This private show would surely continue act by act. For the first dance, they still wore their transparent tight clothing. In the next act, they wet their clothes by throwing themselves into the swimming pool.

They climbed out of the pool and continued to dance. The view was of course somewhat different now. Behind their transparent, tight and now wet clothing, their athletic and well-toned bodies protruded rather more obviously.

The show was reaching its climax. The three men began removing their clothes piece by piece. First of all, their T-shirts came off, revealing their wide chests. As they did so, the dancers went up to some of the women who were now standing around the swimming pool.

Having seen this performance, I suddenly remembered a café called JJ in Kuningan, where a Ladies Night was frequently held. In that event, male dancers would dance on a bar in front of hundreds of guests, most of whom were women. The dancers at JJ wore only a pair of briefs to hide their vital parts. Their bodies were covered with oil. They mingled with the crowds of cheering women and their erotic dance movements would elicit a very hot response from the women, some of whom would shout at them hysterically.

However, the dancers at our private party were, in fact, even more dashing with better physiques. No sooner had I finished recalling the show at JJ café when in front of my eyes the show entered the most exciting act.

The dancers withdrew together, retreating far away from the crowd of guests into the dimly lit area to the left side of the swimming pool. Slowly they removed their briefs, while still dancing sexily.

At this time, to be frank, I felt a little embarrassed. The three male dancers were wearing no clothes at all and their bodies were glistening wet due to the water. In front of around fifteen guests, who were mostly women, they continued to shimmy from side to side. Meanwhile, some of the women offered encouragement—some cried out shyly while others responded hysterically.

The more tipsy of the ladies were even bolder. They were dancing right up to the men, trying to imitate their movements, while still drinking. When one of the male dancers approached her, Ms Rie welcomed him by dancing with him in a very close and intimate position.

If such a show was performed in front of three or four women in a closed room, it perhaps wouldn't have been unusual. In some entertainment places in Jakarta, male strippers were provided, but again, such things were conducted behind closed doors.

I was therefore quite surprised at such an open performance. Everything was like a dream. Except it wasn't a dream, it was real.

The party ended before midnight with the three dancers sweating from their exertions, as were some of the female guests!

It wouldn't have been easy for a woman to obtain the services of the male strippers, certainly not as easy as it was for a man seeking female dancers. The way the male strippers got their bookings was a little different, as they had no permanent base. Ms Sus had ordered her dancers from a beautician, called James, a twenty-eight year old from South Jakarta. James ran his own parlour, SH, in Kebayoran Baru.

James left the day to day running of his beauty parlour to his staff and only did private consultations himself. Ms Sus and Ms Rie were two of the rich women who'd asked James to become their private beautician. It was from this starting point that the availability of the cowboy strippers had been revealed.

The dancers were associates of James, and he was effectively acting as their agent. The fee charged was above average. Ms Sus had to pay around Rp7 million (US$700) for the striptease dance that we'd just witnessed.

But the men weren't just dancers. For an extra fee, they would also be gigolos for the night. This was where the real business of the cowboy dancers lay. They were not only very good at tempting women with their sexy dances, but also skilful in giving a full service in bed. It was this that took place later at the private party at Ms Sus's house.

When the party was over and some of the guests had retreated into their own imaginary world due to imbibing too much wine, lust was still raging. I didn't get to hear what happened next in the luxury house, nor did I know which women claimed the three dancers for rest of the night.

Well, this is the face of our country, the face of Jakarta. It may be right when some of my friends jokingly say: 'Jakarta's become a city that no longer recognizes what is sin.'

I wonder, is that true?

Disco Fever

An international-class discotheque offers VIP rooms for those wanting some private partying on the side, and escorts, who are more than willing to join the ecstacy-fuelled ride.

A room large enough to hold five thousand people throbbed and hummed to the high-volume assault of techno music. On Saturday nights two or three thousand guests jostled for space, dancing and banging their heads to the deafening music. The deep rumble of the bass could be felt in their chests, but the assembled masses didn't seem to care as the dancing continued long into the night.

At the round tables adjacent to the bar and next to the dancefloor area, hundreds of eyes were observing the other guests. The rhythm of the music was infectious; even the seated couldn't help but move their bodies to the beat, as if they were still on the dance floor.

The party wasn't planned with a theme as such; this was just another night in the life of LM discotheque in West Jakarta. LM was always full. A room half the size of a soccer field hosted an assembly of happy, merry dancers, partying the night away.

The guests had paid as much as Rp35,000 (US$3.50) just to get in, although this wouldn't have included the cost of the drinks and certainly not the drugs. Another party was also held upstairs where about twenty-five rooms were available for the extra services.

From within these special rooms, laughter could be heard, mixed in with the husky voice of a singing man. In one room some couples were dancing while gazing into the distance. The large windows allowed the couples to see the action on the dance floor below.

The party had already begun at ten o'clock. My friend and I were deliberately keeping our car under the speed limit, along Gadjah Mada Street in West Jakarta. It was very easy to find LM because it was located near the business and entertainment centres in the city centre.

The entrance lane was already full of cars queuing to get into the parking lot. The LM building was in the same complex as some shops, but seeing as most of these had closed at nine, it was safe to assume that the traffic waiting was indeed for LM.

Security guards with uniforms bearing the LM logo looked tired and bored as they repetitively let in one car at a time. However, we were keen to get in and see what LM had to offer.

After parking up, we stepped into the lift along with several other guests; most of whom I noticed were foreigners. As we approached the entrance door of the club, we could see two security staff wearing safari clothing. We were soon told that the entrance charge was Rp35,000.

The atmosphere inside was fantastic. The golden LM logo shone brightly under the lamps, its motif also engraved within the cream walls of the room. Statues sitting in each corner added to the Mediterranean décor. The stairs to the first floor were made of black wrought iron, complemented by a dark brown floor. Some ornate and colourful flashing lights lit the whole area.

Before departing for LM we'd made an appointment with a young executive named Ronald. He was the twenty-nine-year-old son of a retail businessman who had outlets all over Indonesia. We deliberately chose a table near the entrance door, far away from the loud music coming from the dance floor.

Not long after we'd sat down, Ronald arrived. The guards at the door, who seemed to know him well, greeted him respectfully. We exchanged pleasantries and then accompanied Ronald up the stairs to the first floor. Ronald told us he'd booked a VIP room.

Besides the music and the exclusive interior, these rooms were the star attraction at LM. Our VIP room was ten metres wide and was equipped with a bathroom, some chairs, a table and two 24-inch televisions. Those who preferred their privacy away from the manic activity on the dance floor, found their sanctuary in the VIP rooms.

As soon as we entered, a waitress immediately presented the food menu and drinks list. A woman wearing a black jacket then approached us. I wondered who she was, but soon realised that she was, in fact, a mammy.

She offered us some girls who would accompany us in the VIP room. Ronald nodded and the woman left us quietly. It seemed that she knew Ronald as a special guest.

While waiting for the girls to arrive, we enjoyed the Chinese seafood that had now been provided. Some melancholic pop music was playing on one of the televisions, while on the other TV we watched a fashion show from Paris.

The mammy came through the door accompanied by ten girls. Three of them were Malay while the other seven looked to be of Chinese descent. They stood in a row in front of us, obviously shy but still smiling. I thought that I could see one or two of them smiling directly at Ronald who of course had been here before.

All of the girls were wearing black clothes, some of them wearing miniskirts and transparent blouses, while the others were sporting tight trousers, T-shirts and leather jackets.

Ronald asked us to choose the girls we liked. We giggled nervously but then decided to let Ronald handle everything.

He whispered something to the mammy, who then asked five of the girls to leave the room. The girls left behind were all Chinese. I thought that five was more girls than we could cope with but then I realised that two of Ronald's friends had yet to arrive.

Well, we now had our own little party, laughing, joking and drinking with the girls. The fun lasted for a little while until Ronald's two friends arrived to join in the proceedings. They both chose a girl each.

Three of the girls, we discovered, were called Carol, Aling and Icha. I took to these girls straight away, as they had so far seemed nice, friendly and chatty. Aling and Icha were both twenty-four years old, while Carol was a little younger at twenty-two.

While Ronald and his two friends were absorbed with their partners, we were sitting on the sofa getting to know Carol and Aling. The party for our little group had definitely begun, what with us singing together, laughing and joking, all the while gulping down more and more alcohol. The girls were flirting with us, their tempting behaviour no doubt part of the daily ritual for these professional ladies. Their tips would depend on the success of the evening and if they weren't successful in attracting our attentions fully, then they would be out of pocket.

From our small talk with Carol and Aling we found out that most of the girls who worked at LM were Chinese and that there were nearly a hundred of them working here at various times.

I wondered if they had a display room and asked Ronald about this. He shook his head. He suggested we ask the mammy if we wanted to know more about the girls at LM. We agreed, so Ronald summoned her. She wasn't long in arriving.

She listened intently to her VIP guest as he gave her some instructions. Ronald explained that we wanted to see the full collection of LM's girls and also the other services that were on offer.

This, evidently, was no problem. We left the room with the mammy and took the stairs to the dance floor. By now it was midnight but the place was still buzzing. The throbbing house music was so loud it was hurting my ears. We slowly sifted our way through the throng of gyrating bodies and eventually reached a door marked 'staff only'.

Wow! Soon after the door was opened, the view was a little overwhelming. We saw dozens of girls wearing black clothes. Some of them were joking and laughing, others were enjoying the programs on TV. Most of the girls had Chinese faces. There were of course some Malay-looking girls, but not many. We thought there must have been around forty girls inside the room. Most of the other girls were out in the VIP rooms doing their jobs (this was understandable because on Saturday evenings a lot of girls were booked). It occurred to me that I'd never seen so many sexy girls in one place.

Our presence in the room was certainly unusual for the girls too, some of whom were looking at us rather oddly. Not all guests were allowed to choose their partners as directly as this.

We couldn't stay any longer in the special room as the activity of booking transactions was going on from minute to minute. We moved aside for some mammies who were bringing their protégés back into the room. At any one time, a mammy could be ushering four or five girls to or from one of the special VIP rooms.

We decide to head back. It now seemed that the dance floor was even more crowded. It seemed to be harder to carve a path through the crowd. We couldn't help but bump into people as we tried to find a way through.

I marvelled at all the guests in their switched-on state. It seemed to me that everyone had reached a permanent state of euphoria, no doubt aided by ecstasy! Or maybe some of them were just drunk.

Entering the corridor on the first floor, we found a different situation. Along the corridor, were some guests who were standing in line at the iron railing. Meanwhile, in the crowded VIP rooms, we could hear the voices of male and female guests who were avidly involved in their own parties.

In order to be able to use the room at weekends, a guest had to reserve it the day before. It wasn't surprising to me that all of the rooms were fully occupied. Some guests had tried their luck by booking rooms on the spot. This meant that these guests had to wait for the other guests to leave before they could take their turn.

The VIP rooms on the left and right sides seemed to have markedly different characteristics. The VIP rooms on the left, which directly faced the dancefloor, became special rooms where the guests could be 'switched on'. They enjoyed a clear view of the thousands of guests below them.

In these rooms, the guests could also choose the girls as their partners. The girls could also be invited to enjoy the ecstasy-bound paradise, flying high together with the guests. This scene revealed to me the zeal of men and women who had been shackled by drugs.

Meanwhile, in the VIP rooms on the right, the rooms were specially prepared for guests who wanted to just relax and drink alcohol, accompanied by beautiful girls. We were in one such room.

We held our breath when we saw Ronald and his friends together with their partners. We could see at least three bottles of wine, a bottle of tequila and two bottles of Chivas Regal on the table. No wonder they looked drunk! The songs they sang were merely adding to the fun of the party.

I could tell that, compared to Ronald and his friends, the girls were more sober. Given that they were there to do a job, perhaps this wasn't surprising. It also meant that as long as the male guests were drinking, the more likely these girls were to get a generous tip.

Fortunately, Carol and Aling were not really involved in Ronald and his friends' craziness. It seemed that they had been faithfully waiting for us to come back. Long discussions with the girls continued as we drifted into the early hours of the morning.

In another corner of the room we could see the couples fully absorbed in each other, as if they hadn't seen each other for a while and were now trying to make up for lost time!

The women working at LM principally had a job that wasn't too far removed from the ones of many other ladies of the night around Jakarta.

At SD, which was not far from LM, for example, in the VIP room the guests could enjoy not only facilities like karaoke but also other kinds of service like sexual gratification on the spot. In addition the guests could also enjoy live striptease dancing from the ladies. All of the women in these venues also offered the standard waiting service to relieve the guests' of their inevitable night thirst.

At the ME discotheque they also provided a VIP room for karaoke. The women not only gave very special service to the guests but also offered a package of bedroom services, which was of course done away from the discotheque. A similar thing occurred at DG, which was situated in the Kota Tua district, and at KB, located in Surdiman Street, where the women offered an international-standard striptease dance.

At LM, it was different. There was no striptease dance, except if there was a special order. But the girls at LM were ready to accompany the guests in being wired on drugs until the early hours of the morning. Another distinction of LM was its girls, most of whom were Chinese. The sex service wasn't actually performed on the spot, but it doesn't mean the girls refused to do such a service in another place. In their free time, they usually accepted outside invitations from the guests coming to LM.

Carol admitted that she only worked four days a week. On the other three days she chose to stay in her rented room in a multistorey house. On her days off, she said, she usually accepted other offers that were a bit more special.

'If not accompanying the guests to have dinner, I at least get asked to go out in the city with them,' she said.

Most of the guests who booked her were members at LM. Some guests were even the loyal clients of an entertainment place where she had worked before.

Carol said that she'd worked as a night lady for a fairly long time.

In the beginning, she worked at MJ, a pub-cum-karaoke bar, as a singer. There she worked as a singer not in the solo sense, but as a singer who accompanied the guests when they wanted to sing in the karaoke room but were a little too nervous to sing alone.

'But lately the number of guests has been dropping. By chance, there was a job available in a new place, so I moved there,' she said.

While working at MJ, Carol, who had shoulder-length straight hair said that she only wanted to accompany the guests who were from the same ethnic background as hers, i.e. Chinese. She would make an exception if there were special guests who promised to pay her much more money.

But finally this habit changed permanently because the guests who went to MJ were now extremely varied. The number of Chinese guests was the same as the number of local-indigenous guests, so like it or not, in the end she accepted bookings from any man.

After moving to LM, most of her loyal customers still booked her. Even though the tariff at LM was a bit higher, it didn't matter to them. Because her daily expenditure was increasing she began to accept the extra orders, which was definitely more promising in terms of her remuneration.

Well, guests are guests. Their requests are also quite varied. According to Carol, the guests sometimes ask for weird things. Not all of the guests wanted sex. Some of them just wanted company when having dinner.

'Well, whatever, no problem. The important thing is the money,' she said.

A similar thing also happened to Aling. She'd now become accustomed to the world in which she was living and working. She said there was no difference anymore between her work conditions and her daily life.

Aling, who had really wanted to become a model, had to finally become a night lady because her own needs and the needs of her family, who lived in the Mabes district, were increasing all the time. In the beginning she had just followed her friends into the night world.

Usually, her friends had lots of guests who wanted to be accompanied when they went out. From discotheques, karaoke centres to gambling dens, it was her friends that became the starting point for Aling to begin traversing the nightlife.

To begin with, it was nothing special, but accompanying the rich guests to gamble, or to go to discotheques, was more enjoyable because usually they didn't care about sex. When she'd accepted her first order, she emphasised that she didn't offer any kind of sex service.

From this side job, Aling admitted it gave her welcome extra income. It was her pressing need for money that made her decide to pursue the job professionally. Even though she was only a senior high school graduate, her wide associations made her more mature especially in terms of communication. This could be seen from her natural ability in easily socializing and mixing with the multi-ethnic guests.

At first she worked at the SR Club in Mabes. Like Carol, she worked as an escort for the men who wanted to do a karaoke number. She'd worked at SR for almost two years before she finally decided to work as a freelancer. Two of the venues she worked at were DG and ME; as a freelancer, she could work more independently because she'd built up a pool of repeat customers.

In the end, one of her friends invited her to join her at LM. Enticed by the exclusiveness of the place and its generous salary, Aling accepted and she became one of the official escort ladies at LM.

Aling had of course now changed. As a professional, she was ready to serve and treat a guest like a king. This means that she would do whatever the guest wanted as long as it was in line with a clear business contract. The service she gave at LM was, of course, limited to accompanying the guests when they were high on drugs, or when they wanted to have a karaoke.

Outside of LM? Well, she also accepted some orders that she considered very personal. But still, the guests weren't just anybody. She only accepted the guests that she knew well. One order that she always refused to accept was being a striptease dancer.

'Honestly speaking, I'm not brave enough to do this kind of order. I'm ready to give other services if the pay is great, but not this one,' she said. 'If a guest wants to have a karaoke in one place, he usually calls me first, and then he'll pick me up.'

While Carol and I continued chatting, Ronald and his friends were getting crazier. I didn't know how many drinks they'd been knocking back. Aling and three of Carol's friends, had nearly lost their self-control, such was the amount of alcohol that had been consumed.

By now it was already three in the morning. The music at LM was roaring at super-high volume and party-goers, dripping with sweat, were still in the clutches of disco fever.

Burespang, Burescin, Bureskor

Indonesia's passion for acronyms extends even to the world of sex workers. Burespang, Burescin and Bureskor are terms used to describe waitresses working at certain Japanese, Chinese and Korean restaurants, who supplement their waitressing tips with afterhours services.

It was one o'clock in the morning and the Melawai district of South Jakarta was still bustling. So crowded, it resembled a fairground. Taxis queued for passengers spilling out of the karaokes, while private cars kerb crawled the many side streets and parking lots. The area, which was famous for its night entertainment centres and especially for its Japanese, Chinese and Korean restaurants and karaokes, was dressed up like a night virgin.

From the door of DS club, appeared three gorgeous girls. They were Dona, aged twenty-four, and Risca and Yanti, both twenty-three. My goodness, all three were hot! Dona was wearing a miniskirt and a striking shirt. Risca was wearing jeans and a lace tank top, which exposed her navel, while Yanti wore a tank top and tight trousers. Her hair was hanging loose, covering her slender shoulders.

These were no teenage girls leaving a fashionable café, nor were they three young friends heading home from the disco. No, they were Burespang girls, their first job for the night over and the second about to begin.

Pleasant laughter was heard. It seemed that three men had been waiting patiently in a car.

'Hello. Are we leaving now?' asked Dona, while letting herself fall onto the car seat.

Various types of vehicle were sitting in the parking lot, from minibuses to luxury cars. Besides Dona, Risca and Yanti, there were also scores of other girls who had just finished work. Some of them climbed into taxis, others chatted outside as they snacked on streetfood offered by the sidewalk vendors who occupied almost every inch of the pavement.

As other cars were coming and going, it was evident that most of the drivers and passengers were men. With sharp eyes they looked around, scanning the beautiful girls. We heard them bargaining and inviting the girls into their cars. At the same time, more men came out from the karaoke bars, their partners in tow, and went directly to their private cars.

This early morning scene depicts the reality of life for the Burespang girls of Jakarta. The word Burespang is derived from 'Bubaran Restoran Jepang', taken from the name of the Japanese restaurants that were just closing for the night. This had become a standard term for men who were looking for an adventurous night with a good-looking young girl.

For men, such girls were easy pick-ups. They were known to have double professions. Firstly, they worked as escorts or waitresses in karaoke restaurants and bars. More importantly for these men, their second trade was sex work, and they were ready and willing to trade their bodies for money.

During the day their job was serving the guests who came from all the countries in Asia—from Japan, Korea, Taiwan and China. Not forgetting the Indonesian men who also became their loyal guests. Their main task was just serving the guests on the sofas and making sure they spent their money on drinks as often as possible.

The girls were allowed to eat and drink with the guests as long as it was within the limits of acceptability. Basically they were prohibited from getting drunk.

In the Melawai and Mangga Besar districts, after the restaurants were closed, these girls were now ready for their second job; waiting for the queuing cars, in which the men were ready to invite them to enjoy a passionate adventure.

The johns even had their own slang to describe these girls. 'Burespang' stands for 'Bubaran Restoran Jepang' or 'after the Japanese restaurants are closed'; 'Bureskor' stands for 'Bubaran Restoran Korea' or 'after the Korean restaurants are closed'; and 'Burescin' stands for 'Bubaran Restoran Cina' or 'after the Chinese restaurants are closed'.

These waitresses were different from professional prostitutes who provided a full-time, professional sexual service. These waitresses could perhaps be called amateurs or, more precisely, part-timers, meaning that they didn't necessarily offer their services every night.

Not all of the girls who came out of a Japanese restaurant could be propositioned. In terms of choosing a john, they were very selective. They didn't accept offers at random. Usually, they preferred men whom they already knew or members of the clubs in which they worked. It was much safer for the girl if the man was a member of the club.

For Dona, being a waitress in a Japanese pub-cum-restaurant was more profitable than in other restaurants. When Dona left her hometown of Palembang in Sumatra to seek more opportunities in Jakarta, she first worked in a regular restaurant. There, her monthly salary, including tips, did not even reach Rp1 million (US$100).

'Such an amount of money in Jakarta is nothing,' said Dona, who liked wearing sexy clothes.

As soon as she began working at DS pub, she knew she could earn much more money. DS was full every night with men from Japan, Korea and China, all of them promising great fortunes. She said that the tips that the guests gave to her were bigger than her monthly salary.

'Well, everything depends on us and how well we seduce the guests. The better we are at it, the more we get,' she said. The more money a guest spent on food and drinks, the bigger the bonus she would receive.

'Tips aren't counted by the cashier. Thankfully they go directly to our pocket. It would be impossible for them to end up anywhere else!' she laughed.

What about sexual services? Dona admitted there was always a demand for sex, but she didn't have to perform with every guest who requested it. Even if the final goal was money, she was able to choose whether she wanted to go ahead or not.

'If a guest wanted to pay 100 or 200 US dollars, I'll except it, even if the guest isn't good looking. You know, it's impossible to refuse that kind of money,' said Dona, who I couldn't help noticing had big breasts.

With a little bit of persuading, she said she would consider going all the way if her daily needs were increasing.

'Well, it's not always necessary to end up in bed. In a karaoke bar, if we are smart, we can still get a lot of money,' she added.

It was different for Risca. This twenty-four year old, who was born in Jakarta, was categorized as a prima donna at MJ, a pub-karaoke centre in Melawai. Even though she wasn't particularly tall, Risca was undeniably sexy. Therefore, she also had her fair share of admirers.

'Most of them are from Korea and Japan,' she said.

Risca openly admitted that while working as an escort, whose job was essentially that of a waitress, it was not uncommon for her to accept jobs after hours.

'Provided the request is acceptable, then why not?'

Having a beautiful face was advantageous for Risca. She was frequently asked to accompany a guest abroad. Lately, for example, she'd been asked to go to Singapore for three weeks, and during that time, she was paid daily, according to the fee that she'd determined before leaving.

'I asked to be paid 100 US dollar a day. Well, that was like one night's income if I worked at MJ,' she said, justifying the price.

At MJ itself, she worked as a freelancer, so that she didn't have to work every day; she was under the supervision of a mammy, who looked after her working hours.

'It's as easy as that. Only if there's a booking do I have to turn up and look after the client.'

Everyone knows a restaurant is a place where people go to eat and drink. A Karaoke is a place where people can sing while watching TV. But if a restaurant is combined with a karaoke—especially if it's a Japanese, Korean or Chinese establishment—its connotation could be different. At such places, a guest is able to eat, drink and sing but also partake of extra services. Sexual services.

Business is business and restaurants could not, of course, survive without waitresses. But their customers would abandon these Japanese, Korean and Chinese karaoke restaurants if the waitresses didn't also provide extras.

It's quite possible that the turnover generated by the waitresses was even greater than that obtained by the restaurant management. The waitresses existence could be categorised as underground prostitution. Formally, their job was to accompany the guests, to chat with them and also to keep them drinking. What was unofficial was the sex service.

The activities really began at nine in the evening. The waitresses themselves started working at seven. The working hours in Japanese, Korean and Chinese restaurants differed slightly from other restaurants, which usually opened earlier in the afternoon.

Not all the waitresses were registered as official employees of the restaurants. The numbers of wait staff officially registered in the Department of Labour and the number of the waitresses working in the restaurants was always very different! Most of them worked as freelancers—Yanti, for example, took advice and directions from the manager, allowing her to do her job when she was required.

Incredibly, despite Indonesia's monetary crisis which has been worsening over the years, the girls' income was not decreasing. In fact their income was *increasing* due to the exchange rate of the rupiah against the US dollar. Most of their tips were in US dollars or other foreign currencies, especially Japanese yen and Korean won.

But what else would you expect when most of their guests were businessmen from East and Southeast Asia, as well as East Asian expatriates living in Jakarta. Once in a while, they might even get a group of sailors from China, Japan or Korea.

The circulation of dollars in some karaoke joints was significant. Chaca, a twenty-four year old, who worked as a waitress in a Korean karaoke restaurant called MSK could earn enough money from her profession to buy a house, land and a private car.

Yanti also experienced the same thing, never leaving her cell phone behind when going anywhere. Wherever she went, a driver always picked her up. The money she earned in one night could reach hundreds of US dollars. If the money was converted into Indonesian rupiahs, the amount would reach hundreds of millions.

Some waitresses said that their income was more than enough. Adek, who worked as a waitress in a Japanese restaurant called LL, said that her income wasn't stable though; it went up and down every night.

'Because the money was given as tips from the guests it isn't totally stable,' she said. Her tips were mostly in US dollars. 'Well, on average, I get about US$50 to 100. Once, a guest gave me US$300. And US$100 is worth one million Indonesian rupiah!'

Adek's comments were corroborated by twenty-five-year-old Ivon, Adek's colleague. The divorcee, who had a child and was still very striking, said that the average tip she pocketed was between Rp200,000 (US$20) and Rp500,000 (US$50).

'I never got more than Rp500,000 (US$50),' Ivon explained, adding that she only expected that kind of tip from regulars. She continued with a slight chuckle, 'The cash I got was frequently in US dollars. Seldom did I get any yen or won. You know, for the time being, the dollar's a bit higher.'

According to twenty-one-year-old Susi, the money in circulation at HL karaoke restaurant in Ancol was very big. In one night she could accompany three to five guests. On average, her tips were between US$100 and US$200.

'Well, we just need to be smart when it comes to making the guests happy,' she said openly.

I asked whether it was just a case of accompanying the guests when they were eating or drinking in the restaurant.

'No, of course not!' replied Eka, a nineteen-year-old friend of Risca and fellow waitress at the Korean MJ in Melawai. According to Eka, while her main job was indeed sitting with the guests in the restaurant, after that, it depended on the agreement between both parties.

'If the pay is big, then why not give more?' she reasoned.

The easiest way for cash-rich customers to relieve themselves of dollars and donate them to sexy young girls was to seek out the karaoke restaurants. The three main locations in South Jakarta, which were always full to bursting with foreign men ready to spend the sexual dollar, were Melawai, Block M and Mangga Besar (Kota). And of course there was always Ancol. The Melawai district at night was a totally different animal to the that during day. Before nightfall, Melawai was chock-full with everyday sellers and traders. But when night fell, Melawai became altogether more exciting and lively.

There were about ten restaurants that were full of ladies of the night. Some of them were situated near the Golden Truly department store. Others were near the former Sepatu Roda (roller skate) discotheque, or next to BCA bank. In the daytime most of these restaurants opened for only a few hours around lunchtime. After that, they closed until about six. Even by seven in the evening there were only a few guests to be seen in the restaurants.

From the outside, some of the karaoke restaurants looked like any other restaurant. But many had tinted windows, and looked dark or closed. The front doors were always shut, as if the restaurants did not accept guests. The only signage, which indicated that they were indeed restaurants, was written in Japanese or Korean.

The restaurants in these three districts were really different to those in the Pluit area, which were more open. During the day the restaurants in Pluit were usually very busy. The restaurants in this area were also places where a family could have lunch together. Some restaurants even became highly regarded because of their food!

Most of the restaurants in the Pluit area catered to Mandarin-speaking guests, either those who were expatriates, or businessmen from Taiwan, Hong Kong, Macao and China. Some of the restaurants and karaoke bars deliberately limited their operational hours in the style of a curfew.

However, as the desire is strong, even these curfews have been known to be broken.

Gay Pride

A group of homosexual men is invited to a frivolous cross-dressing high-society party. In a country where homosexuality is not illegal but also not encouraged, especially among the elite, are the gay men there as friends, for entertainment value or merely to boost the hostess's shock value?

We had attended gay parties before, either in a discotheque in MG street, West Jakarta, or at LJ café in South Jakarta. These fun parties of flirtatious men were held on a regular basis, if not publicly advertised. It was here that homosexual men hung out with friends, and looked for partners.

But this time, a gay party was being held in a private house. We knew the owner, a respectable woman named Mrs Erika. She was thirty-one years old and ran several elite boutiques in Jakarta. Her husband, Bagus, ran a business importing and exporting car spare parts.

'This is a private party and limited to certain people. It's called Gay Night Party 2002,' confirmed Mrs Erika when I enquired about her special gathering.

On Saturday night at ten o'clock, a friend and I were in DL street, an elite settlement in the GT district. The house we found ourselves in was designed in the neoclassical style and was surrounded by a wall four metres high, with a wooden gate that featured a carving of a lion.

In the eighty-square-metre living room, which had been converted into a ballroom, about twenty guests were already mingling.

This was a party with a difference though. The female guests were made up like men while the male guests made themselves up like women. Had it only been gay men we would not have been so confused; we could barely recognize our hosts!

Mrs Erika, who was well known on the local celebrity circuit, was wearing men's clothes: a white shirt and black trousers with a bowler hat, and she sported a false thin moustache above her upper lip. Her right hand was clutching a walking stick, while her left hand held a cigarette.

Her husband, Bagus, was wearing a white tank top with a cloth wrapped around his legs, and bright red lipstick. Other guests were similarly attired.

'Tonight we're swapping gender. If you want to join in, there are some clothes in the bedroom,' said Erika, giggling.

We were bubbling over with enthusiasm. What a unique party. Out on the garden terrace, there were at least a dozen female guests, but they weren't ladies, they were actually men! All of them were made up like women but their way of speaking was graceful. The scene was further confused by at least five real women who had made themselves up like men.

Among the invited guests were three interesting guys who had dressed up to impersonate Hollywood stars. Erika introduced the three of them to us as Jojo, age twenty-four, Raymond, twenty-six, and Priambudi, twenty-nine. There was another guest that she introduced to us named Anton.

Jojo was a fashion-show regular, a former winner of a cover boy contest some years previously. The pale-skinned man, who always looked trendy, was commonly known to be gay. The gossip about his relationship with a famous designer was a hot topic in the mass media and amongst his fellow models.

An opportunity presented itself before the party began for Jojo to talk to us about his relationship with the famous designer. He said that he was still sad because their relationship was not running smoothly anymore; in fact they'd recently broken up.

'My man was seduced by a *lekong* [guy] in Block M,' he said angrily. 'Compared to me, that guy was nothing. He must have seduced my man.'

Meanwhile, Priambudi had worked as the assistant to a well-known designer for about three years. The dark-skinned and well-built man ran his own business. He said that he'd recently decided to split from his boss and go it alone.

'I was in Africa for one year,' he said. 'In the last few months I've been preparing an international fashion show. It was Nelson Mandela himself who requested the show. For the time being, I'm on holiday here in Indonesia.'

Unlike Priambudi, Anton wasn't a model but every day he hung out with male models like Jojo and Raymond who were two of his closest friends.

In their daily lives, these three friends behaved like any heterosexual man and no one really knew that they were men who preferred someone of the same sex.

At first glance, they were toned, handsome and always tried to appear gentlemanly. What made them different from other men was perhaps the way they talked. Their voices were sometimes more graceful and softer. These characteristics were more pronounced when they talked among themselves.

However, this night, Jojo, Raymond and Priambudi had all changed into women and looked convincingly female. Their style and appearance, which in daily life often displayed feminine characteristics, looked perfect when they made themselves up this way.

The party began with a dinner and then continued with the opening of several bottles of red and white wine. To the sound of RnB and classic disco, the guests were soon swigging the drinks until there was nothing left.

'Drink as much as possible! It will get you nice and relaxed!' encouraged Jojo.

Ten minutes later, two couples appeared at the front door. Erika introduced them as her younger brothers and their wives. Like Erika and her husband, the two couples had dressed up in reverse. The other guests laughed uproariously at this sight.

The dinner and drinking lasted for about one hour. When it was almost eleven, Erika invited all the 'contestants' to gather in the living room. As they gathered together, the sight that greeted us was quite odd. Our first thoughts were of the men who hawked themselves every night in the Taman Lawang district.

Having said that, the three men in front of us were quite different. Jojo wore a lady's traditional outfit from Solo in Central Java: a *kain* or long piece of cloth covering his lower body combined with a *kebaya* or long-sleeved blouse held together at the front with broaches. Meanwhile, on his head was a bun adorned with a jasmine flower. He looked like a Javanese princess. His lips were beautified with red lipstick. In his hand he held a fan that was decorated with a flower motif.

In the other corner of the room, Raymond was dressed like Madonna in her film *In Bed with Madonna*. In keeping with the film, he had deliberately let certain parts of his body be visible behind his costume.

Priambudi was dressed up like Cher, the singer. He was wearing a black gown with fur accessories and a V-shaped cut in the back. The bravest was Anton. He was only wearing a black bikini like Demi Moore in her film *Striptease*! His dyed blonde hair was offset by his black lipstick.

The other guests were also daring in their attire. One of them had dressed up exactly like Brooke Shields, while a dark-skinned man, who was standing near Jojo, bravely attempted Pamela Anderson. I didn't know how his breasts could be made to appear so large and protruding behind the pink dress he was wearing.

Erika's husband and her two brothers still looked shy. In fact, the three of them were also entered for the contest, which was divided into two categories. The first category was for those who chose to take part in the catwalk contest, and the second was for those who preferred to lip-synch along to certain songs.

Before starting the contest, Erika introduced three jurors who would assess the contestants' performance. Someone had told me the first prize was a one-week holiday in Hawaii.

At a quarter past eleven, the catwalk contest began, but not before all of the contestants had first gone up the stairs to the first floor. Some minutes later, about twelve contestants began, one by one, to strut model-like down the stairs. Popular songs like 'Mambo No. 5', 'Bailamos', 'If You Had My Love', 'No Scrub', 'Genie in the Bottle', 'Lady' and 'Take Me Home' accompanied them during their stroll down the catwalk.

This was exactly like watching a real fashion show. Jojo, who worked as a model anyway, walked gracefully, swaying his hips stylishly. He waved his fan theatrically as he progressed down the catwalk.

The other contestants followed suit. Erika's brothers and husband joined this first session. They were still pretty shy but they did their best, even though theirs was more of a cameo appearance—their routine lasted less than two minutes but fun was had by all.

The second contest was awesome. Now the show was really kicking off. At first, Raymond appeared, accompanied by Madonna's song 'Take A Bow'. With an erotic dance, Raymond expressed his style very well, all flirtatious and wild. When the song was almost over, he began to remove his clothes piece by piece. The only clothes still attached to his body were his bra and briefs. All of the guests shouted hysterically as Raymond's performance ensued.

Dressed up like Cher, Priambudi acted while singing 'Believe'.

Through his V-backed dress, now open wide, sweat was flowing freely. The accessories twisting around his body wobbled, and some of the furs on the accessories fell off and spread over the marble floor. The guests repeatedly cheered him on as he began swaying like a vulgar striptease artist.

Amidst the cheering, Jojo took a glass of white wine and moved toward the middle of the room. He approached Priambudi with a fulgent smile. Priambudi clearly welcomed the white wine, gulping down half of it immediately. He then poured the rest of the wine all over his body. His sweat mixed with the wine leaving the onlookers agog and eyes wide.

Anton's antics then became the climax of the gay party. Accompanied by house music, he performed a striptease. Wearing only a bikini, he looked exactly like the professional exotic dancers found in the many less salubrious entertainment venues around Jakarta. From inside one cup of his bra, he proceeded to remove a package of liquid. With a slow and sensual motion, he began smearing the liquid all over his body. Once in a while, his hands pulled at the mini shorts that covered his lower body. He approached some of the guests as he did so, dancing provocatively.

Anton entertained the astonished party guests for about ten minutes with his performance. Erika, who was sitting with her brothers, couldn't stop laughing.

At the stroke of midnight, Erika asked all of the contestants to stop their activities. They then gathered to form a circle. Led by Raymond, they began praying to signify the end of 2001.

'Even though today we have been dressing up like this, we believe that God does not merely look at our appearance, but into our heart as well. Hopefully, we'll be happier and more successful in 2002.' This was more or less the content of their prayer.

This retrospective moment didn't last long. In the next instant, the music and laughter exploded again. Even though the contest was over and the contestants were waiting for the results to be announced, the music was playing and the guests were swaying to the rhythm.

It was then that a famous female singer, MA, who had released several pop hits in 1998, appeared at the front door. She was about to release her new album in mid-2002. MA was a welcome addition to the party.

Jojo, Raymond and Anton seemed to know MA, who after saying 'hi' to them, then immediately joined the crowd of guests. The only person who hadn't changed her gender for the evening was MA herself as she'd just finished singing in a café in Jakarta.

In order to welcome MA, Anton and Raymond staged a wild, vulgar dance. Seeing this, MA burst into laughter until her eyes were wet with tears. While Anton was doing his erotic dance, two men who were wearing trousers and tight T-shirts now appeared at the front door. Jojo, Priambudi and Raymond immediately welcomed them and it turned out the two guys were Anton and Priambudi's partners.

Seeing his lover arrive, Anton stopped his dancing and, still wearing his bikini and drenched in sweat, passionately kissed him. Laughter, music and the clinking of glasses were to be heard until early the next morning.

Anton was smiling happily because he'd won the contest. A ticket for a one-week holiday to Hawaii was already in his hand, as he was sitting with his lover on a sofa. Meanwhile, Jojo, Raymond and Priambudi had won Rp3 million (US$300) each.

'Not bad. At least this money can be used to cover the cost of our make-up and clothes,' said Priambudi.

Jojo, Raymond, Priambudi, Anton and the other gay guys at the party expressed themselves so freely. They were free to behave however they wanted. Often, homosexuals are forced to conceal their way of life, but what we saw at the party was refreshingly different. Erika, together with her husband and brothers, gladly opened themselves up for this group of people.

At this party, they were accepted for who they were. They were allowed to express themselves without the differences in sexual orientation being a barrier.

In terms of social status, the three friends hailed from wealthy families. Jojo, Raymond, Priambudi and Anton had no problems in terms of money. Every day they could go anywhere by car, have a meal or drinks in top cafés and it was no drama to be wearing branded clothes. But in terms of their social associations, they liked to gather around those who had the same sexual preferences.

It was not about being brave or not if a man like Jojo liked being among his own group. For Jojo, what he did with his contemporaries was not exclusive.

'It doesn't mean that we know nothing. People like us aren't fully accepted by some people,' he said.

According to Jojo, in Eastern culture, homosexuality is still considered a little weird and is often viewed as a deviant behaviour, which challenges uncomfortably the existing norms.

'Who is the person who wants to be born like me? If I were asked to choose, I would also want to be like other straight men,' he continued.

Raymond and Priambudi also proposed similar feelings. They admitted that the realization of being homosexual had begun long before now.

'This is not exactly like going along with whatever happens to be the prevailing fashion,' Jojo continued.

If their existence couldn't be accepted by society, then they could only submit to their fate.

'What can we say? Here, in our society, who is the man who frankly admits that he is gay? At the most, there's only a handful. In our society, gays are not accepted yet. We don't want to be exiled either,' they said.

The gay party that Erika held was for them considered a kind of honour or validation. Nevertheless, Anton said, they were also God's creatures who needed the same treatment as everyone else in society.

'If a person like Erika wants to accept us, it's a great appreciation for our situation,' he said.

Perhaps.

It could be that Erika was one of the only wealthy, respected women who *could* accept the presence of a group of gay men. Or maybe she just wanted to hold a party that was different from other parties. Thanks to her, any parties attended by her colleagues would not seem strange anymore!

Scissorless Barbershops

Going for a haircut and a blow-dry in some parlours in Jakarta is merely a cover for meeting and arranging dates with sex workers.

Health parlours and salons abound in Indonesia and for the vast majority the services they provide are legitimate. These fashionable parlours have a regular and plentiful clientele, and are popular with young executives and trendsetters.

Naturally, as well as these ordinary salons, a new type of parlour has emerged, offering special services. Such a parlour not only offers hairstyling, blow-dries and facials, but also a special package for young men who like to be pampered all over.

These parlours have special menus that offer treats that are indistinguishable from standard sexual transactions. The parlours are always busy, frequented by beautiful girls and handsome men, the type of people who would also hang out in trendy bars and cafés anywhere in Indonesia.

One of the salons offering a special package for men is known as CA parlor. Actually, I happened to visit CA on the invitation of my friend. Bayu, a twenty-nine year old, worked as a project director in an advertising agency.

The comforting services on offer, such as massage, seemed to be a valid form of relaxation for a busy man burdened with the burnouts, tiredness and stresses of city life. Therefore, when Bayu invited me in one afternoon to relax at CA parlour, I readily agreed.

'Want a massage? You'll get it. Fancy a herbal cosmetic treatment for your complexion? You'll also get it. Whichever you choose, it's up to you. Both are very pleasant,' said Bayu when we arrived at CA.

I couldn't yet fully appreciate why Bayu chose to visit CA parlor. As I was standing in front of the reception desk, all that I knew so far was that CA wasn't merely a parlour or salon, but that it was also equipped with other facilities for massage, as well as a steam room and sauna.

CA parlor was situated in Kebayoran Baru, or more precisely in TH Street. CA was on the first floor of a three-story whitewashed building.

The parlour occupied a room that was about ten metres in width on the right side of the first floor. Meanwhile, the left side was equipped with a steam room and sauna. On the second and third floors, several rooms were fitted with air conditioning. Some of these rooms were sufficiently well allocated to be considered VIP standard.

The services offered by CA were like any other parlour, but the difference was that at CA there were no male staff. All of them were beautiful females, wearing purple uniforms.

Besides having been famous as a massage centre, CA was better known for the special packages given by the parlour officers. Seen from the facilities provided and the price, CA could be basically categorised as an exclusive parlour.

Therefore, it wasn't surprising that those who went to CA were mostly men from the middle and upper class. This could be seen from the various models of cars parked in the carpark. The cost of one treatment was very clearly different from the cost in other normal parlours. One package of a cut, blow-dry and facial cost Rp100,000 (US$10). This excluded the cost of the herbal treatment.

It was this type of special service that gave CA parlor its exclusivity.

It seemed that a man like Bayu had become accustomed to the special packages provided by CA. He said that of the numerous treatments offered, his favourite was the herbal cosmetic treatment. The service given was not merely limited to the herbal treatment, but it was more than that, a more accurately titled 'full' or 'in-out' herbal treatment.

'Several friends call it "triple-X herbal",' laughed Bayu.

The treatment package usually related to a sauna service. So, before having a sauna, the guests could ask for one of the beautiful parlour girls to do the herbal treatment. A special room had, of course, been prepared for this facility, the safety and cleanliness of which were guaranteed. This room was no more than three metres in width.

For more privacy, some guests preferred the VIP rooms. These rooms were not only bigger but were equipped with bathrooms as well. None of the other rooms had en-suites.

The special package of herbal treatment was popularly known as triple X herbal treatment. The term 'triple X' was actually meant to depict the peak of the herbal treatment practice itself when the guests could give their passion free rein.

'The logic is that the treatment covers all parts of the body, without any exceptions. Just think about it, what's going to happen if a man and a girl are behind closed doors? Well, what else if we're not dealing with sex,' said Bayu, trying to explain.

And as one of the customers of CA parlour, Bayu knew what he was talking about. Even though the triple-X treatment was more expensive than a massage, there were still plenty of men who were very keen on this service. The official price of the package was only Rp145,000 (US$15). If a guest wanted to add the sauna package, he had to pay as much as Rp45,000 (US$5) extra.

In order to get the triple-X package, the request did not go through the receptionists because only some of the parlour girls provided such a service and only when already behind closed doors with the customer. The prevailing price was usually no less than Rp300,000 (US$30) to

Rp400,000 (US$40) for a complete package of triple-X service.

At least, that was what Vivi, one of the parlour girls working at CA had said. She had indeed known the risks of working in a salon from the very beginning. The job was fairly risky, especially for a beautiful girl like her. For just over a year working at CA, Vivi, who was from Manado in Sulawesi, knew exactly what was involved when she faced the horny male customers. But she continued to conduct her profession freely.

'All jobs are risky,' she said.

The risks Vivi frequently faced were that the guests often asked her to make love with them.

When she'd worked at CA for the first time, she was prepared for everything. In the beginning, she limited her work to washing hair, blow-drying and facials. Eventually, however, she came to be offering the herbal cosmetic treatment to men, which was a whole lot more personal. Nobody else was in the room but her and the man.

Vivi could certainly be categorised as a beautiful girl, so it wasn't surprising that she became a prima donna at the parlour. Standing 165 centimetres tall with straight black hair, Vivi attracted a lot of interest from the guests. There were many men who wanted her to serve them.

'They're all familiar with the in-out service now,' she said.

Having dipped her toe in, Vivi reasoned she might as well jump straight in. Due to a worsening economy, she could no longer refuse an invitation to 'pom pom', the coded term used by girls working in a parlour that means offering sex behind closed doors.

'Anyway, pom pom is not a secret any longer,' she said.

Offering the full pom pom service enabled Vivi to earn at least Rp300,000 (US$30) to Rp500,000 (US$50) in a single day.

If CA was famous for its triple-X treatment, then PY was known in Jakarta as a rendezvous for short-time dating. PY parlour, at least among young people, attracted quite a lot of interest. Its outlets were spread throughout Jakarta.

The PY parlour was not a grungy place, but was well known as a clean and tidy salon. The service it gave was the same as the other parlours in general, from hairstyling, blow-drying, manicures and pedicures to, perhaps, a herbal treatment.

One of the PY parlours in South Jakarta—located in a Block M mall—became a centre for young people to hang out at. The mall itself was located in an area that, at night, became the base for dozens of male and female streetwalkers who were waiting for customers.

It seemed that these professional prostitutes became permanent fixtures at the mall. They even had their own special hangouts, one of which was PY parlour. During the day they deliberately went to PY in groups to have a beauty treatment or just to chat with their friends from the same profession.

The large number of 'professionals' who hung around at PY every day eventually enticed some adventurous men to visit the place. Not only did local men come to the parlour, but Western ones as well. The main draw, the prostitutes, ensured PY was always a lively venue.

The sex-hungry men always requested the special treatment once inside the parlour. Inside the room the prostitutes usually made the first move by making some blatant hand signals. In order to confirm a transaction, the men usually dealt directly with the target. But some first-timers used the help of the salon officers who doubled as matchmakers.

The intimacy between the sex workers and the salon officers could be clearly seen. Relaxing talk and laughter frequently filled up the fully air-conditioned room. The salon, in practice did not officially provide an extra service; in fact it could be thought of as a rendezvous point between men and the prostitutes.

If a sex transaction was to happen, it wasn't always between a man and a woman. Indeed, it wasn't unusual for a man and a man to go together, as well as two women. Such a sex transaction, which occurred between couples of the same sex, was nothing out of the ordinary. This was because besides being the base for women offering extra services, PY had long been famous as a known centre for gays.

From noon until late afternoon, the hired girls were usually window shopping in the mall for fun or looking out for new customers. At night, they hung out at a restaurant in MM street behind the mall. Here they traded their services openly by standing in the street waiting for a man who might want to book them.

I talked with Jay, a member of staff at PY, who understood the behaviour of the clients. With his graceful way of speaking, Jay said that most of the men who liked beautifying themselves in the salon did not only want the beauty treatments.

'Many of them really come here for the sex,' he said.

Working at PY for about two years, Jay even had several members tell him frankly what they wanted. Jay said that soon after the guests arrived in the salon and saw some girls talking amongst themselves, they would directly ask him whether or not they could take the girls out. If the answer was yes, Jay then became the matchmaker for the guests so that they could enjoy a sex transaction with the girls.

'On average, most of the male guests who come here are up to some mischief. But not all of them are like that,' he continued.

His profession as a matchmaker was quite profitable. For each transaction, he could make money from both parties—the guests and the girls.

'I get some money from the guests, and the girls usually give me some money when they've done the job,' he explained.

According to Jay, so far, PY had merely become a place where the guests and the girls could make a date. No more than that. After they got the partner they wanted, the men would continue their date elsewhere based on the agreement between both parties.

'Based on what the girls say, the guests usually take the girls to a hotel,' he said.

Jay admitted that it was normal for a lot of guests to come to the salon with a side purpose.

'Such are men. Who doesn't need sex? Even me, you know. I love men,' he said candidly.

When asked about the image and reputation of the salon for providing girls, Jay said that he didn't really care about that. The reason he liked the parlour was besides being famous as a salon where people found sexual partners, PY was also popularly known as a place where gays met.

'Let people say what they like. The important thing is that this place does not provide a direct sex service,' he affirmed.

If CA provided the triple-X package and PY was popularly known as a place for arranging dates and follow-up transactions, then FL salon, located in the Gunung Sahari district, was famous as a high-class salon.

What was interesting about FL salon was that its girls were a cut above the rest. Seen from their pretty faces and sexy physical appearance, they were definitely much better than even the escort ladies working in some elite karaoke centres in Jakarta.

I could only shake my head in disbelief when Yan, a friend of mine, and I dropped by at one such salon specifically to see if this was true. Yan had helped me quite a lot in terms of providing me with the newest information about the nightlife in Jakarta. Working in PR and marketing communications for a company dealing with artist management meant it was easy for him to make acquaintances with lots of people from the night world. Not to mention his side job as a model and television actor. Even though he had never had any leading roles, he was often recognised by the public.

On that afternoon, when Yan invited me to find out the truth about the fabled FL salon girls and I couldn't really refuse.

The building housing FL was quite large and sat on the same street as some offices and shops. Its parking lot, large enough to take about twelve to sixteen cars, looked fully occupied. Yan and I had to park our car quite a way away from the salon.

Once inside, we could feel the comfort of FL's interior. The living room was equipped with a long sofa and a glass table. There were about ten girls who were conducting their job, serving the guests, all of whom were men. Some of them were cutting hair, others taking care of a manicure or pedicure. But some others were merely having a relaxing chat while gently massaging the guests' heads.

Yan and I were the eleventh and the twelfth clients in that afternoon. Two beautiful and very sensual girls served us. They were not wearing uniforms like most salon staff, but wore trendy, street clothes.

It was not surprising that most of the girls working at FL were beautiful. In fact, FL not only operated as a normal salon but also was a place where guests could have sex. Amazingly, all of the girls working at FL were ready to accept a booking.

The services such as facial massages, hair styling, manicure and pedicure were actually no less than a way of introducing the clients to the girls they wanted. Even if the guests didn't continue on to a date, the tariff for the massage alone would be more than Rp200,000 (US$20). No wonder that most of the male guests at FL that afternoon came in luxury cars.

'Only having a facial, Sir? Don't you want to invite me out for dinner?' whispered Wina, who was serving me that afternoon. It was from Wina that I began trying to unravel what FL salon was really about.

Who could refuse the invitations of a beautiful and sensual girl like Wina, who was tall, pale and had a lovely figure?

For one date, a guest had to pay Rp1 million (US$100). That didn't include tips, the cost of a hotel room, dinner and so forth. No wonder then, that FL was dubbed a high-class salon.

Judging by the behaviour of the men who came to the salon that afternoon, it was clear that most of them were regulars. Having finished their treatment with one girl, the men continued to chat with the neighbouring girls. It seemed that the guests and the girls already knew each other; or at least that there had been a transaction before.

Yan extended his massage with an all-nighter.

'I'm just curious to try it. To see whether or not her moves are good,' whispered Yan while laughing.

Besides CA, there was also another salon in Wijaya, called ST salon, which also provided triple-X service. ST was established in a shopping and office complex, so that it was easily located. The girls who offered the triple-X treatment were mostly former massage girls. The girls at ST not only gave treatment, but were also willing to be invited to make love with their guest, depending on the agreed fee.

Solo is not that different from Jakarta. Famous for its slogan, 'Smiling Solo', the city is bursting at the seems with parlours and salons offering a similar full service.

Once, some time ago, we visited Cipto Mangunkusumo Street, in the Tunisari area. Situated there was YL salon, which was not only popular among the men in Solo but was also well known by those from further afield.

In this salon, run by Ms YY, there was not much chance of getting a haircut, blow-dry or facial for YL didn't even have any salon equipment like scissors, salon caps and other necessities.

So, what did it serve? Well, nothing other than the services of women who could satisfy a man's hunger for sex. The way it operated its business was not much different from the one applied by some other entertainment venues in Jakarta.

When the guests arrived, Ms YY's procurers, all of whom were men, would gather all of the girls and ask them to wait in the display room, which was about six metres wide. The girls sat on a U-shaped sofa. The guests were free to choose the girls they liked. In the first session, Ms YY would display six girls. If the guests could not find the appropriate girl, her procurers would display the second group consisting of six girls, and so on.

As soon as the guests found girls they liked, Ms YY's procurers would offer transportation to take the guest and his partner to the place of their choice. YL did not provide rooms; it was no more than a place for booking services. The tariff for one short-time date was around Rp200,000 (US$20) to Rp300,000 (US$30), excluding transportation costs. To help the guests find suitable rooms nearby, Ms YY's procurers provided a list of short-time hotels.

The chosen girls could either be taken out there and then or they could be delivered later on. Everything depended on the guest. Regular customers could even order the girls by telephone. Of course, for newcomers, it was better to go directly to the salon to see Ms YY's newest and best offerings.

The girls on offer were not like the average Solo girl, who is always very graceful and polite. These girls were more like entertainers in Jakarta, dressing provocatively in trendy clothes. This was quite understandable since most of them were not originally from Solo at all. Most of them actually came from other regions like Ngawi, Boyolali, Madiun, Sragen and the other surrounding areas. Some of them hailed from outside East Java, like Central Java or even as far as Kalimantan.

The situation at YL was not like that of other massage parlours in Jakarta, where the guests had to wait their turn to have a date with a girl in a dating room that had been provided. At YL, if there were four to six guests present at any one time, then this was already considered a lot. This was because the guests who came to YL liked to cash and carry—they came in and then left with their purchases.

The flow of guests through YL was very fast. Noticeably missing was any kind of comfortable waiting room; it was even difficult to get a soft drink there. Rarely did the guests hang around for long.

To help the guests better observe the available girls, there was no partition between the living room and the display room. The guests could observe the girls for as long as they liked. If necessary, the guests could have a chat with the girls to get to know them better. Again, this was different from what was usually found in Jakarta, where the girls were displayed in an closed glass-fronted display room, or fishbowl.

There were many different salons offering sex services in Solo. It's said that such places may be found in almost every sub-district of the city. Evidently the business of selling sex from parlours is common to most big cities in Indonesia. There is no real difference between Solo and Jakarta, both of these cities present similar faces. The faces of big cities plastered with the powder and lipstick of girls ready to be of service.

Super Mammies

Presiding over a network of girls—and sometimes famous models and actresses—are the super mammies. Former sex workers themselves these industry matriarchs keep a tight reign over their business assets.

In the sex trade, there is one necessary link between the punters and the girls. A connection is needed to bring these parties together. These mediators, or maybe in modern parlance, agents, are known by many terms: GM, procurer, broker, or if they are female, a mammy.

These procurers play a very dominant role of determining the recruitment process, marketing their clients, and arranging the final sale. It can be said that they are the trump card that must be played in each game.

As far as procurers go, the name Hartono once caused a significant stir in public arena. This infamous international procurer had thrown Bali into a tumult with his mega project Bali Planet. This was a high-class entertainment venue in which there were hundreds of beautiful women available to be booked at one's leisure.

What remains of Hartono now, might only be his name. The latest news about the man from Surabaya was that he had many problems, one of them related to his house in Darmo Street.

The house had become the subject of a lawsuit. Hartono's frustration got the better of him when he finally decided to set the house on fire. In an article released by a national newspaper, Hartono said that he'd become a poor man. Therefore, it wasn't altogether surprising when people said that his era as a big GM was over.

Hartono's story is just one of hundreds though. Many other stories tell of procurers who've done very well from their operation. Understandably, a large percentage of successful GMs, or procurers, are women.

On a smaller scale than the Bali Planet, several venues in Jakarta offered the services of prostitutes. Most of the GMs organizing these girls were female. At the LM discotheque, in Hayam Wuruk, all of the five supervisors were women.

These procuresses were busy ladies, covering a wide territory and looking after a lot of girls. In general, they acted as their managers, sorting out their dates and fees for them. In practice, like at the DK parlour, in the Grogol district of West Jakarta, around 300 women were under their supervision. Usually, one mammy supervised around fifty to a hundred girls at any one time.

Just take a look at the distribution of finances prevailing at the DK parlour. The basic tariff was Rp80,000 (US$8) per hour or Rp90,000 (US$9) for the VIP class. For the smaller tariff, the money earned was divided up as follows: Rp30,000 (US$3) was for the GM, Rp40,000 (US$4) was for the parlour management, Rp2500 (25 US cents) was a 'security' expense, and Rp7500 (75 US cents) was paid in cash to the girl.

From this simple breakdown, the dominance of a GM can be clearly seen. The GM received more money than the girls did. Even though the Rp30,000 (US$3) to the GM was supposed to be held as savings for the girls, all deposits, withdrawals and interest were still under the GM's control.

The problem was that even though the Rp30,000 (US$3) was

supposed to be a kind of guarantee or fall-back for the girl, in reality it acted more as a bond to keep the girls there.

The sex workers at DK were accommodated in a big house owned by the broker. This might sound easy but in fact this was anything but a free ride for them. The rent was taken directly from their income and the broker tightly controlled and supervised everything that the ladies of the night did.

If one of the girls wanted to go shopping, she had to be accompanied by a driver. In fact, wherever the girls went, they had to tell their mammies. Outside of working hours, which were between two in the afternoon and four in the morning, they had to stay in the house under close supervision.

One of the prostitutes at DK was Wiwin, a twenty-four-year-old woman from Malang in East Java, who had been working at DK for more or less two years. Wiwin admitted that she became a charge of Mammy Tien, who was then thirty-eight years old. According to Wiwin, there were at least twenty-five women who lived together under Mammy Tien's control. It was Mammy Tien who structured their lives and job.

'Everything is handled by Mammy Tien. If I want to buy powder, she must know about it and she always guards me. Not to mention when buying luxury things like jewellery,' said Wiwin frankly.

In a house called 2xx, in the Hayam Wuruk district of West Jakarta, Joyce, a forty-two-year-old madame, was also prosperous. She had run a brothel for about five years and had at least twenty-five charges.

Joyce ran her business successfully. Every day dozens of men came to the house to look for a sleeping partner. With a tariff of Rp350,000 (US$35) for one short-time service, Joyce sought out men from the middle class as her clientele.

In fact, Joyce's house merely functioned as a place where clients could negotiate a transaction. Nothing more than that. The facilities of the house included a wide parking area that could accommodate around eight cars, air-conditioned rooms and a fairly luxurious interior. It was in the living room, where a guest was welcomed and asked to choose the girl he liked. Usually, it was Joyce herself who coordinated the process until an agreement was reached. Soon after the deal was made, the guests paid in cash on the spot and after that they could take the girls out to any place they liked.

For one short-time transaction, the tariff was Rp350,000 (US$35). But in practice, there were lots of guests who booked the girls for a longer time—from one night to several days. The tariff for the longer bookings was usually around Rp750,000 (US$75), but climbed as high as Rp2 million (US$200). In one day, Joyce could broker about five to ten transactions.

Joyce's girls varied in age, with several older ones on the books.

'The eldest is twenty-eight years old. Actually, there are only two or three women who are that age. The others are still very young,' said Joyce.

When calculating how much money Joyce earned from doing this, one thing was certain, her business was very profitable. With only five transactions in a day at Rp350,000 (US$35) per booking, the total amount of money she could earn was easily Rp1.75 million (US$175). Taking into account the long-time transactions and she must have been pulling in tens of millions of rupiah.

The picture presenting itself was that of a rich woman. Joyce still looked beautiful and lived together with her two children. Without a husband, she had two members of staff and three servants who helped her to run her business. A BMW 5 Series was parked in the garage of her house. One could always see her wearing luxury clothes and accessories, and her daily appearance was always immaculate. Everything she was wearing was branded, from her clothes and her watch to her shoes.

Some of Joyce's girls lived in her house, but others lived in an apartment she rented not far from the main house. Even though most of the girls were freelancers, between ten to fifteen women would be standing by in the house from midday.

An exclusive album was placed in the living room of the main house, so that the guests could also select their partners from the photographs. So, if a guest couldn't choose a girl from the house, they could choose from the extra girls on stand by.

Joyce's business network was not only limited to that particular prostitution house. She was also a wide-ranging supplier of girls to karaoke bars and other entertainment venues. In RM karaoke bar in Ancol, for instance, Joyce supplied at least twenty girls who were ready and willing to serve the guests, even ready to sleep with them.

For the horny men of Jakarta, Joyce's was not a new or strange name. Before becoming a mamasan, when she was still young, Joyce used to be a player herself. When she was still a fresh-faced beauty, Joyce was well known as one of the prima donnas among the high-class call girls.

Besides Joyce, another prominent procuress in Jakarta was Mammy Irene, a forty-three-year-old Chinese Indonesian woman. She had many girls who were spread between three massage parlours in prominent hotels in Jakarta: the TL hotel in Central Jakarta, and the AR and GL hotels in South Jakarta.

In these three venues, Irene supplied at least fifty massage girls. The girls were employed on rotation and moved between venues on a weekly basis. Based on rough calculations, the average fee per hour for the massage service at TL hotel was Rp125,000 (US$12.50), while at AR it was Rp115,000 (US$11.50) and at GL hotel Rp132,000 (US$13).

Almost all of Irene's girls were ready to give the 'service plus'. This meant that they were not only trained in professional massage, but were also prepared to provide sex directly on the spot, or outside their working hours.

For a transaction outside working hours, a girl had to give Irene Rp200,000 (US$20). Therefore, the average price demanded by the girls for one transaction was above Rp300,000 (US$30) for a short-time service. For the massages conducted in the hotels, Irene received a twenty-five percent commission for each transaction.

A number of mammies targeted their businesses towards higher-end clients, offering well-spoken girls who also worked as models or artists. One lady making a fair profit doing this was Sisca, a thirty-one-year-old single girl from Bandung.

To begin with, Sisca had run a modelling agency, which then developed into an outlet providing young, beautiful girls to rich men. Most of the girls on her books, aged between eighteen and twenty-five, were not yet well known as models but their age and appearance meant that Sisca's girls were proving very popular with the rich businessmen in Jakarta.

Sisca, who lived in a house in Tebet, South Jakarta, supervised at least twenty models from Jakarta and Bandung. In the luxury house, which was also used as her office, Sisca ran her sex business. The agency was only a small part of her overall business activities. Sisca had two permanent staff who helped her run the modelling agency, while Sisca herself ran the prostitution ring.

Almost all of the operation of Sisca's business was centered in Jakarta. A typical transaction followed two steps. First, as soon as a client ordered a girl on the telephone, Sisca would make an appointment to see the client and take over two or three girls to meet the man.

'If the guest orders one girl only, at the most I bring two or three girls. So that my client can choose the one he likes,' Sisca told me.

Most of these appointment with the clients took place at a dinner or lunch setting. It was then that all the transactions were concluded, including any cash payments. Sisca had two categories of models. For the A-list models, the price for one night was Rp5 million (US$500). For the B-list girls, the price was Rp3 million (US$300).

Despite the high prices, the pool of clients was bottomless, and many of the clients were repeats. On one day, Sisca could broker two or three jobs. For a A-lister, Sisca earned Rp1.5 million (US$150), and for a B-lister she took Rp1 million (US$100) per job.

As well as Sisca, there was another mammy who played the celebrity hooker game. Febby, who came from Surabaya, used to be an actress herself and had starred in some popular films. Her face had also been a regular feature in the print media up until the mid-nineties.

In her glory days, with her sexy features and beautiful face, Febby belonged to the category of Indonesian actresses known as '*bispak*', an acronym of '*bisa dipakai*' meaning 'available for use'. Rich Indonesian businessmen were not unfamiliar with Febby's name and availability. Commanding a price of Rp10 million (US$1000) per job, Febby was able to enjoy a comfortable life, befitting an actress. She owned a Toyota Corolla and a large house in the Cibubur district.

After having a child and going through a divorce, Febby changed her profession. Since she was still close to numerous celebrities, she became a matchmaker for other *bispak* actresses, willing to sleep with rich men for money. Sometimes Febby also served clients who still wanted to sleep with her.

Febby was then a successful broker, a matchmaker to the rich and famous. Two of Febby's actresses-cum-prostitutes were KY, a television actress, who once threw the Indonesian film industry into a tumult with her raunchy acting, and AY, a very famous star whose face is regularly seen on television. Both actresses were ready and willing to accept overnight jobs with Febby's help. With a price tag of Rp25 million (US$2500) per night, Febby confirmed that a lot of rich men were vying for their services.

Febby was free to determine the price for each job. It would not have been unusual for her to push the price up from twenty-five million to thirty million rupiah for some clients. For such a job, Febby would take home Rp5 million (US$500).

Febby's approach was very simple. When the clients called her and wanted actress X, Febby then contacted said actress. Febby would invite both parties to dinner. It was during the dinner that all the business was handled.

Such meetings, according to Febby, were also aimed at avoiding all of the things that an actress might be afraid of.

'If they recognize the man who books her, you know, it can be a nuisance,' said Febby, who now has access to at least fifteen famous Indonesian celebrities.

Money seems to be easily earned by the procuresses. This is a business that always makes plenty of profits and the matriarchs of Jakarta are very wily at conducting, and controlling, their operations.

Truth or Dare

In a conservative society, were there are limited avenues for sexual exploration among young people, a simple game such as Truth or Dare takes on greater significance.

Late into the night, raised voices could be heard coming from a nearby room.

'Keep on opening it. Come on, open it. Don't be shy!'

The noise was coming from the suite of a four-star hotel in GT Street, South Jakarta.

Now, a little shriek was heard, followed by silence, then indistinct muffled talking could be heard. Soft music was playing in the background. What I saw next were two naked girls dancing shyly in front of their friends.

Meanwhile, in the early hours of a Monday morning, in a room at the Bunga Apartment in East Jakarta, the action was even more daring. Two men and three girls were playing cards in a private room. Each of the players picked up one card in turn. Whenever one of them held a card saying 'truth', a candid and truthful story had to be related to the others. When the word 'dare' was spelled out, the holder of the card was challenged to a physical activity. When the girl got the dare card, the men would ask them to remove an item of clothing. Sure enough, she would soon be naked. Although this started out as a fun game, it wouldn't be long before the tone of the evening would change.

My colleague and I hadn't visited the Bunga Apartment (serviced apartments in the Cempaka Putih area) to specifically see this scene. It all started when Bertha, a newcomer model whose face could be seen in some tabloids and entertainment magazines, invited us to go to her apartment.

'I'll introduce some friends of mine to you. They're really beautiful, and they're OK people too,' she said jokingly.

Bertha was an easygoing person, who could make friends very quickly; we knew her from the MA café in Surdiman Street. As a newcomer to the artiste world, the twenty-two year old from Surabaya was friendly enough and very active. She liked to have dinner with friends or just hang out at fashionable cafés.

We were in ZB café in Block M and Bertha was accompanied by her female friend, who was also charming. Bertha introduced her as Susi, who was twenty-four years old. It was then that Bertha invited us to have dinner with her the following night.

We weren't going to refuse a dinner invitation from a beautiful girl like Bertha, although we were a little surprised that she asked us over to her apartment and not to a restaurant.

Bunga Apartment was situated in a main street, not far from a by-pass connecting a foreign franchise supermarket with a big intercity bus station. The apartment was pretty luxurious with a modern interior. The main entrance to the building used an electronic keypad system. Even though it was already after eight o'clock in the evening, the area around the apartment was still bustling. Several food outlets were open.

We took the lift to the ninth floor and stopped at the door marked B/93. Bertha came to the door wearing a long pink dress and she gave us a warm welcome and invited us to take a seat. Already present were three guests: two girls and a guy. We knew one of girls, Susi. The other girl was

Dona, who was twenty-one. The man introduced himself as James.

Susi, who lived on the seventh floor, wore a tight blue T-shirt and smart trousers. Dona, a tan-skinned girl with a mole on her forehead, wore a knee-length, purple dress. Dona explained that she frequently overnighted at Bertha's apartment and James often came along with her if he had nothing better to do. James, who was said to run a transportation business, often hung out with Bertha.

'Hey, you know this isn't a real dinner,' said Bertha as she joined us in the living room.

On the walls of the room were hung some large photos of Bertha. Some of them showed her wearing sexy clothes in rather sensual poses. There was also a 29-inch television and a CD and VCD player.

As the evening progressed, Bertha served us with some fine food. We thought that such effort was unnecessary for a social dinner in an apartment. As we finished off some tasty grapes and pears for dessert, I noticed that it was now nine thirty.

Bertha showed us around the apartment, which had a distinctly pink hue. It was a studio flat, with two main rooms, the second of which faced the street and was where Bertha slept. On the pink walls of her room was a black-and-white photo of a nude woman. The photo was artistic and didn't show the subject's face.

'That's me three years ago,' said Bertha.

Having done the tour we gathered again in the living room. This time, we deliberately chose to sit on the carpet, as Bertha, Susi, Dona and James were also doing the same.

'Hey, instead of doing nothing, why don't we play cards?' said Bertha suddenly.

We nodded our agreement. Why not? we thought. When it came to playing cards, we weren't great but not totally stupid. Our friends were just sociable youngsters who were also fond of playing cards, either just for fun or to gamble.

Susi, Dona and James also agreed with the idea.

'At least, we have something to do,' said Dona shyly.

We found ourselves sitting in a circle on the carpet. Bertha changed the channel of the television to find one of the non-stop music stations. Bertha told us that the name of the game was Truth or Dare.

The Kings represented a dare while the Queens meant truth. These were shuffled into a regular pack of cards. Having heard about the game, we were of course curious, and it turned out to be quite different from other card games we'd played.

Whoever got the dare card had to be ready to do anything. Whereas if you got the truth card, you had to be willing to tell a story about something, usually of a very personal nature. These were the rules.

As we played we listened to songs by the likes of Jennifer Lopez, Madonna and Britney Spears. Bertha became the dealer, deftly distributing the cards. Each player got one card for each of the three rounds respectively.

It was in the third round that every player had to show the card he or she was holding. If there happened to be no truth or dare card, then the cards would be reshuffled and distributed again until one of the players got one.

However, there were some people who played the game without cards. Usually, the game was played by pitting one's palm against the palm of another. The upper palm meant dare and the lower palm meant truth. The rule was that the players had to guess when their hands were pitting against each other until their guess was correct.

To begin with, the game was bringing up fairly mundane questions. When Bertha and Dona got the truth card for example, we would just ask them simple stuff like their ages, their weight and their height. The same thing happened when we got the dare cards, the girls asking us to squat or to hold our noses.

But the longer we played into the night, while drinking wine and beer and eating snacks and fruit, well, the hotter the game became.

Finally, the tension was released. Dona received a dare card, and James, Bertha and Susi asked her to stand up. Bertha then asked her to begin dancing and to untie her hair as she did so.

In the next moment, Susi asked Dona to remove her tight T-shirt. Dona surprised us when she immediately did what Bertha and Susi had asked. Now she was only wearing her bra. My goodness! This was a surprise. Although we'd been invited by some rich friends of ours several times to watch striptease dancing, it still manages to startle you when it happens in front of your eyes!

For a while, Dona stopped dancing and we continued the game. Usually, the rules of the game stated that the winner was only allowed to propose one request. No more than that. Therefore, when Bertha happened to get the truth card, we asked her to tell us about her career as a newcomer to the world of acting.

'It's bitter and difficult!'

That was Bertha's first answer. In the beginning of her career, she had to take a 'short-cut'. Starting with a minor role in a film, Bertha had to willingly be 'personally coached' by a film director.

A tragic situation, indeed.

Bertha then started her career as a model by finishing runner up in a fashion contest organised by a beauty product company in Surabaya. Since then, she'd received various modelling offers. She did some work for magazines as well as appearing in advertising and promotional brochures.

In the end, she decided to move to Jakarta because a friend helped prepare the way for her. Her decision to move to Jakarta was also precipitated by her family who had disowned her after she became pregnant and subsequently had an abortion.

Then Bertha received an offer to star in a film, but this didn't necessarily improve things for her. Indeed, every opportunity she got ended up with the same thing—afterhours coaching. That typified her early career. Bertha said that she fell from one man to another. The end result was that she finally got into some television productions and films, even though she was only starring in minor roles.

Her story finished, the game continued. Again, Dona got the dare card. She was now only wearing a bra and jeans, and naturally had to remove the rest of her clothes.

Bertha also got the same dare card. No sooner did she get the card, she immediately removed her dress ... By one in the morning, the two girls were wearing nothing at all. Meanwhile, Susi was wearing only her underwear, and James was only wearing shorts, leaving his chest bare.

We thought that the game was over. We were wrong. In fact the game was getting more and more serious. We couldn't remember how many times Dona and Bertha had acted out lesbian sex scenes.

A similar thing happened with Susi, who had to serve James. The sexual tension in the air had finally transformed the room into an arena that was awash with naughty and lewd behaviour.

The Truth or Dare game had become a fun pastime among younger people in Jakarta. But the game was actually a smokescreen. In the end, it was merely a chance to explore sexuality within the confines of a conservative society.

Shopping Queens

Self-labelling in the world of sex workers is a complex issue. For these high-maintenance girls, who do not consider themselves to be call girls, their clients are their 'lovers', who stay with them for a month at a time. Showered with expensive gifts, have the girls forgotten they are still just selling their bodies?

The procurement methods of call girls are many and varied. Girls working from a house, for example, might receive an order through the telephone via a madame. Some might meet clients directly in a dating place while others rely on repeat customers.

But these girls are a bit different. They are not call girls. They like to be called 'high-class girls'. Such a name describes them as girls who like the glamorous life with beauty as their capital. How do they do it? By hunting wealthy men.

In an elite mall in South Jakarta, two beautiful girls, Maria, twenty-two, and Linda, twenty-four, were walking hand-in-hand with two nattily dressed men. It was about six o'clock, the time when people were travelling home from work. I recognised Maria and Linda from seeing their faces several times on the covers of magazines, but surprisingly I also recognised the two men who were walking with them. I had met them before in various cafés. They were Remy, twenty-nine, and Jose, thirty-one.

I knew that the two men were quite popular among the café community. This wasn't surprising because they were successful young executives. Remy belonged to the board of directors at PT AR, a holding company that was located in SD Street. Meanwhile, Jose had his own car parts business centered in TR Street, Central Jakarta. I heard that he was one of the stakeholders.

For several moments I observed them from a fair distance. The two couples entered a branded clothing store, and then came out carrying bags. After that they entered a watch boutique, soon coming out with Maria and Linda carrying small packages.

I went to greet them as they were having dinner at the LN café in the same mall. LN was very much an elite café, because most of the clientele were executives. Remy and Jose were surprised to see me but still remembered me. They introduced me to Maria and Linda as their girlfriends. My suspicions were aroused and I finally goaded them into an intimate chat.

Maria was a new model whose face was commonly seen on the covers of various entertainment magazines while Linda had acted in at least five television productions. The two of them were easygoing girls who could be quickly become close to other people.

They talked frankly and easily about many topics. They were friendly and assertive and I found no difficulty chatting with them. Remy and Jose also got involved in the relaxing banter, laughing and joking along with the girls.

Five days later Remy and Jose met me again at JC café in Central Jakarta on a Saturday evening. They talked about Maria and Linda whom they acknowledged as their lovers. Actually from what I'd heard about Maria and Linda, they liked befriending rich men. Indeed, I happened to see them several times having dinner with smart guys in swanky restaurants.

But it seemed that for Remy and Jose, such gossip didn't really matter.

'The most important thing is that I am happy, isn't it?' he said, not unreasonably.

Over the following three months, I got to hear about Maria and Linda in detail—how they tracked down their dates, who were of course wealthy men, and how their personal life was.

My relationship with the girls was one without barriers; they no longer behaved secretly or tried to conceal anything from me.

They frequently invited me to have dinner with them in their houses. On one such visit, sprawled on a thick carpet in the living room, I began listening to the story of the two girls. Our talk that evening was focused on men. It was perhaps because they felt close to me that they talked about this without embarrassment.

Maria, who was said to be the daughter of a rich man in Surabaya, told me why she'd come to Jakarta. Maria was being forced by her parents to marry a man she didn't love so, in the end, she fled her home with her boyfriend, Doni.

For the first six months she lived with her lover in a rented house. Maria soon fell pregnant. They often quarrelled, and Maria eventually left her lover and aborted her unborn child. She actually met Linda in a discotheque in Jakarta. Linda worked as a model and it was because of Linda that Maria began to get involved in the modelling scene. Her shapely body and stunning face had brought her into a new world.

For the first few months, Maria lived in Linda's apartment. Maria's sensuality and beauty were her blessings. In less than six months, her face was already being published. Almost all of her poses were sexy and graceful. That was the starting point for Maria to begin acting in films, although never as the lead actress.

Linda was, in fact, not merely an ordinary model. She had a side job.

And it was her side job that earned her a lot of money. As a middle-class model and television actress, her face was now well recognized. Linda was getting more popular and this she used as capital for her side job, namely being a high-class girl.

Maria then followed Linda's lead. The acting and modelling world was, in fact, merely an interim career, no more than that. Maria soon widened her career when she became a high-class girl. The process of running her new profession wasn't complicated; being beautiful, popular and sociable made it easy for her in this line. Also, the frustration of her former lover's actions, meant that Maria was not short on motivation.

The interesting point was that Maria and Linda's profession as high-class dates could be said to be distinctive. They didn't consider themselves to be call girls, but more than that. They did not like being labelled as call girls. In looking for their dates, they did not accept an order over the telephone or with the help of a GM. They themselves looked for and decided whom they wanted to date.

Usually, their modus operandi was that they went along to cafés, pubs and clubs that were known to be somewhere that rich men usually frequented. It was in such places that they inveigled the rich men.

Maria and Linda's dates were not cash and carry one-nighters but frequently lasted for a month or more and they referred to their dates as lovers.

'Mas Edo was an understanding person. He bought me a Bulgari watch, and invited me to go to Singapore with him last week,' admitted Maria.

Maria had been in a relationship with Mas Edo for almost one month. Edo, who wasn't Indonesian but was a Singaporean Indian, ran an automotive business. Maria always accompanied him when he attended a party, had dinner or hosted his business colleagues. To all intents and purposes Maria and Edo looked like a pair of lovers.

'Next week I'm going to Hawaii with him,' said Maria.

On one Saturday evening, I was invited to meet Maria and Linda's new lovers. They'd made an appointment to meet me at CI café, in AA Street, South Jakarta. Maria was Edo's lover no longer. One month had been enough. The most important point was that she had collected a lot of branded goods and had saved a lot of money.

The two men that Maria and Linda met that night were still young, probably in their late twenties or early thirties. They were neatly dressed and looked good. Soon after I'd taken a seat, I was introduced to the two guys, Rick and Bram, as the girls' close friend. At first, I thought that Maria and Linda were still seeing Remy and Jose, but I was wrong. It seemed that those relationships were over.

'One month is already more than enough,' said Linda.

On the table were bottles of expensive drinks. Maria herself was a white-wine maniac, while Linda was addicted to margarita and B52s. Rick and Bram were downing Jack Daniel's.

They spent their time at the café until it closed at three in the morning and parted with at least Rp5 million (US$500) on drinks that night. It seemed that such an amount of money was nothing to them. It was just to treat the girls in the café. After that Maria and Linda were taken home.

'This is our first date. We've known each other for just one week. This is still the try-out phase,' said Linda when arriving home.

The purpose was to see whether or not Rick and Bram were suitable guys to date and whether they could be relied on to be financially generous!

'If we catch the wrong guys, it's a waste of time,' joked Maria, laughing freely.

Maria and Linda reminded me of some escort girls in karaoke centers or clubs who liked being part-time lovers or kept women of rich men rather than accepting one-night bookings. Some of the escort ladies in the karaoke in Melawai Street, South Jakarta, for instance, became the wife-away-from-home of expatriate men like those from Japan, Korea or Singapore. Seen from a financial standpoint, it was certainly much more advantageous.

Maria and Linda invited me to join them again the following week. It was late afternoon when Rick and Bram parked their new car in front of Maria and Linda's house.

Rick and Bram were not like the average man on the street in Indonesia. Like Remy and Jose who were said to have 'money with no serial numbers', they were also successful young businessmen. Rick had a wood-trade business, while Bram himself was successful as a contractor.

I waited for them at the NN café just to taste the tiramisu and the frothy warmth of some cappuccino. Some minutes later, Maria and Linda arrived at the café with their dates. Through her cell phone, Maria had told me that they wanted to do some shopping first.

I stayed in the café listening to Latin music, while waiting for Maria and Linda to finish shopping in the mall. In fact, it wasn't until I had had my third glass of cappuccino that Maria and Linda finally appeared from the lift, accompanied by Rick and Bram.

The girls were fully laden down with expensive looking packages. My God! I could only shake my head. Each bag contained the likes of Versace shoes or Prada clothes. They joined me at the same table and ordered some food for dinner.

Later in the night they invited me to join them at the OL café in Thamrin Street where we enjoyed the live music while having a meal and drinks. This might be the same schedule that Maria and Linda had already followed several times before with their other men.

The girls were sitting on their lovers' laps, looking exactly like two couples that were very much in love. Once in a while, they would kiss each other intimately. They burst into laughter regularly and gulped down drinks ceaselessly. Talking and laughing, with intimate and exciting hugs, the sweet, romantic words poured out. The beat of the music, the tinkling of glasses, and the dim light of the lamps in the café seemed to be like a silent witness.

It was already three in the morning, the time when the guests had to leave the cradle of laughter, the women and the drinks. Everything was exciting and intoxicating. Only a few guests were still drinking in the café.

'We want to check in to a hotel. Want to join us? Don't worry, I'll pay for it,' said Maria.

Maria and Linda, together with their spouses, were walking hand-in-hand. I certainly knew what to do; it was impossible for me to follow them, spending the rest of the night with them. A male bumblebee had found a blooming flower in a closed room.

It was four thirty in the morning when Maria rang me on her cell phone. She had just called to thank me for accompanying them. After that, I was soon sound asleep in my dreams. Alone.

The next day I had tea with Maria. She looked very happy, smiling beautifully as she arrived in her silver BMW. Linda hadn't come along with her as she was having a herbal cosmetic treatment in a salon.

'Rick has invited me to go to the Netherlands. I'm leaving on Monday. He's doing business and having a holiday as well,' she said.

Going abroad meant money—at the very least Maria would certainly get a lot of riches from the trip, meaning branded goods and expensive gifts. Her already extensive wardrobe would no doubt expand further after the excursion.

The dating quickly led to an accumulation of money. A woman like Maria could bring a man like Rick to his knees. Their way of treating the men as lovers for an extended period of time was the perfect opportunity for Maria and Linda to acquire as much wealth as possible. There was no fixed prices because they were no ordinary sex workers.

Maria contacted me again a week later. As she spoke on the phone she was laughing as she told me about her experience in Holland. She had stayed in a five-star hotel, enjoying all its luxurious comforts. This was the life as far as she was concerned.

So was Maria happy with her glamorous life and the way she always changed her rich men? This week, for example, she was in the embrace of a man named Denis. Three weeks later, she will hug another guy called

Sebastian. And in the next weeks, she will hug Jack, Will, and so forth. They might have different names but these men would all be wealthy.

How about the men whose money has been successfully drained? For Remy and Jose, money wasn't really a problem. Remy, for example, had spent more than Rp100 million (US$1000) on Maria, and Jose had spent a similar amount on Linda. Maybe the way to look at it was that both parties were happy. The men got their high-class date for a fee that had no real bearing on their overall wealth, while the girls got all the extras that they so coveted.

'Maria even asked me to buy her a new car. If she was still my lover, she would have had a new Mercedes by now,' Remy told me.

I wondered what Maria's reaction would have been to this news.

Remy said that he was quite happy and that he'd enjoyed his days with Maria. Amidst his busy job as a director at PT AR, a holding company in TM Street, he felt comforted by Maria's presence. Didn't he feel he'd been used as soon as she left?

'I don't care. The important thing is I have got everything I wanted from her. If I lose one, I'll find another new one,' he replied.

On the surface Maria and Linda appeared to lead glamorous lifestyles. This could be seen from the house in which they lived and from the exclusive way it was furnished. The house was located in TTD Street in Tebet, South Jakarta, an area famous for its boarding houses, flats, apartments and elite rental properties. The house undoubtedly looked luxurious and it had a high fence and gate.

On entering the front yard of the house, we could see a small garden with lots of plants and a pond in which there were some large fish. A black Volvo 950 and a silver BMW 5 series were parked in the garage.

'Hey, take it easy. Just make yourself at home,' said Maria, while inviting me in.

In the lounge, there was a pink sofa and a crystal lamp in the middle of the room. A portrait of a woman in a golden frame was hanging on the wall and an aquarium sat in one corner of the room. The floor was covered with a thick fur carpet.

'Don't be shy. Take it easy. You know, it's safe here,' said Linda, who suddenly appeared from the door of a room, startling me as she did so.

It seemed that Linda's bedroom was near the living room. From the stairs, which had white porcelain floors and a polka dot motif, was heard the sound of Maria's footsteps.

'My room is upstairs. Want to see it?' she offered.

I agreed and we went up the steps. Maria's room looked luxurious. There was a big spring-bed with a dark blue bedsheet with a flowery motif. The bedroom was fully furnished with a large wardrobe, a make-up table and electronic fitness equipment. A glass door led onto a balcony, which was in fact a mini garden terrace.

Of much more interest were Maria's photos hanging on the cream walls. All of them showed Maria in different sexy poses. Two of them showed Maria virtually naked. For a moment I was startled.

'Dinner is ready,' called Linda, who appeared all of a sudden.

Linda, with her long hair and sexy lips, was wearing a knee-length dress. Her face was made up, her red lipstick prominent.

Maria left us for a while because she wanted to wash her face and change her clothes. Linda and I were waiting in the dining room, which was right behind the living room.

Seafood and a bottle of wine soon appeared on the table. I was amazed with Maria's house. For models of Maria and Linda's status, having such a luxury house was a bit surprising. How did they earn enough money to buy such a luxury house, expensive furniture and prestige cars?

'Life is false,' said Maria when we were having a chat in her luxury house.

Maria held such bleak views of life because she knew nothing of genuine happiness. The men who made her fall in love had ruined her life and her hope.

That was also the reason why Maria became a carefree girl who enjoyed her life one day at a time. She didn't care about her future any longer. When having a date with a man she liked, she looked strong and self-confident. But of course she was like any other woman—she really needed love and affection.

Maria didn't know when she could end her status as a high-class woman, because at the moment she wasn't ready to leave such a glamorous way of life. Money and men—this is all Maria has known. I do not know what tomorrow brings for her.

'For the time being I just enjoy what I have. I'm tired of thinking about my life. Just be happy. That's it,' she said while breathing in deeply.

Divorced from Reality

Divorced at a young age from philandering husbands, often with children to look after, Jakarta's league of young, rich female divorcees party their lives away.

Shinta was a thirty-seven-year-old divorcee of a businessman who worked in a mining company; Monica, a twenty-nine-year-old divorcee of a man whose father was the former mayor of a district in DKI Jakarta.

The two ladies were very well off but lived in a world of false jokes and laughter. Colourless and spoiled, they hung about the city's cafés, passing the time with no serious purpose. To others it might seem that they were enjoying themselves. Deep in their hearts, though, they cried and screamed. They felt truly alone in their solitude.

Jakarta's divorcees had their own community. Almost every night they attended the ZB café in Block M. They usually reserved a private room that could accommodate up to twenty people. Those who attended were not just women, but also middle-aged and elderly men. The café management considered them special guests—as customers, they were big spenders.

It was from ZB café that I knew Shinta and Monica. Both of them looked friendly, and were easy to talk to.

Usually, along with some of their gang members, Shinta and Monica would spend their afternoons in the cafés like the ones at Plaza Senayan. If not, they often relaxed in beauty parlours, gossiping about everything as they treated themselves to a manicure.

They also had a regular gang for their monthly social gatherings. Sometimes, they met in the local cafés or maybe in their private homes. Of the members of this particular divorcees clique, the person I knew best was Shinta.

Shinta once invited me out to celebrate Monica's birthday. The party was held in the ballroom of a four-star hotel. Arriving early, I decided to take a look at the ballroom, which was on the second floor. Some of the hotel staff were busy preparing and decorating the room. Sweet-smelling flowers were arranged on the dining tables, and a small party bar was set up in one corner of the ballroom, which was twice as big as a volleyball court. A colourful carpet covered the floor, and ornate, gold-coloured lamps lit the room.

Half an hour later, Monica, the host of the party, came in accompanied by some of her friends. Shinta was walking beside her. Monica wore a long V-shaped purple gown, while Shinta wore a knee-length black dress. Her beautiful legs had all the men staring! Both ladies also wore diamond necklaces.

The guests began to arrive. At the entrance door, Monica and Shinta welcomed their friends by kissing their cheeks. Most of the guests were women who were twenty-five years and above. All of them wore glamorous party clothes.

It was not surprising that most of Maria and Monica's friends were wealthy women. Monica herself ran a garment and boutique business for branded imported products. Before she divorced, she was married to a man in the oil business. Meanwhile, Shinta worked as a director in a mining company. From her marriage, Shinta had two children. The first child was nineteen years old and the second was sixteen. Monica herself had a four-year-old son from her marriage.

By nine o'clock, the ballroom was full with guests. Around forty women were mingling, laughing and joking, and about twenty-five, mostly older, men made up their own group.

Among the crowds I could see some high-class Indonesian artists. There was a famous young singer, SN, and a handsome television actor, JT, who was idolized by many women.

A well-known Master of Ceremonies called Antoni (who frequently appeared on television) introduced some erotic dancers who we soon saw were only wearing thin G-strings. They danced for about forty-five minutes with their undulating and tempting moves.

The guests applauded noisily, egging the dancers on. Some men who were standing closest to the dancers tried to beckon over the female dancers. Some of them even tried to dance with them.

The party continued with SN singing three love songs. According to Shinta, SN was Monica's close friend. SN was making a name for herself in the Indonesian charts; Shinta had specially invited her to sing some songs as a birthday gift for Monica.

The cutting of the birthday cake took place at eleven o'clock. The first piece was given to a man named Joseph. I didn't really recognize him and wondered who he was.

'Come on, kiss her. Don't make her wait!' shouted some of Monica's friends.

Monica kissed her man for a long time! Whether he liked it or not, the man, who was handsome enough but a little fat, responded to Monica's kiss warmly. The guests applauded noisily in the ballroom.

'Joseph has been Monica's close, special friend. They've been going out together for about two months,' explained Shinta to us.

The party continued. RnB songs, acid jazz, and even garage music was being played loudly. The tinkling of glasses and the loud music were mixed with jokes and laughter from the guests.

The party became wilder as the night progressed. By one in the morning, there were only around twenty-five guests remaining in the ballroom, most of them were Monica and Shinta's close friends. I was introduced to three women who always seemed to accompany Monica and Shinta whenever they went out.

'This is Marcela, this is Jeny and this is Joyce. All of us are the same. Young divorcees,' said Shinta.

The behaviour of the five divorcees was becoming more daring. The air reeked of alcohol whenever they laughed.

The three new faces were regulars in some of Jakarta's elite cafés. Whenever they attended an event, their bodyguards always accompanied them. It was said that the three of them had become the mistresses of rich Chinese men.

They then began mingling with the men who were still present in the room. JT, a handsome actor, became the women's main focus of attention. Monica, Shinta, Joyce and their friends were behaving brashly in order to attract JT's attention. They bravely attached themselves to JT, repeatedly inviting him to dance, toast and pose with them for photographs. Because JT was known to be a playboy himself, he never refused an invitation. In one exchange, Shinta hugged him, but in the next second he was in Jeny's arms and then Joyce's embrace, and so on.

In the other corner of the ballroom, some couples were chatting intimately. Monica and Joseph, both drunk, hugged each other tightly while dancing even though the music playing was a kind of garage music.

The remaining men, no more than eight in number, who were caught in the crowd of women, became Monica and her friends' obvious targets. The women started to remove their upper clothing, Marcela nonchalantly pulling off her gown until she wore only a thin, transparent bra and panties.

The climax of the party saw the girls modelling together in a hot pose. In their semi-intoxicated state, all inhibitions were gone. Marcela, Joyce and Shinta gamely flaunted their sex appeal, shouting hysterically once in a while as the fever of the night got the better of them.

The attendant hotel staff could only shake their heads, laughing as they observed the girls' fearless behaviour. Some of the guests, who were still too shy to join in, kept silent while drinking and raising their glasses in appreciation of the frivolities.

By three o'clock in the morning, the party was almost over. The only people still in the ballroom were Monica and the gang, JT, Joseph and two men who were Shinta and Jeny's close friends.

After the hotel party was over, they didn't go home directly. In their drunken state, they decided to continue the party at the NS karaoke-pub in Thamrin. This place was still considered a happening venue because it had only been running for one year.

'I've reserved the place. Let's party until tomorrow morning,' said Monica, who was leaning against Joseph's shoulder.

One by one, cars arrived to pick them up, all of the cars being luxury models. Monica was with her man in a dark blue BMW 5 Series. Shinta was picked up with a Mercedes E 23, while, Marcela, Joyce and Jeny were in a Caravel-type car. JT and two other men were driving a Cherokee and a Volvo 960 respectively.

It took around half an hour to drive to NS where Monica had booked a VIP suite. The room was on the second floor, not far from a non-smoking billiards room. Two waitresses welcomed us and immediately provided us with special menus. Three bottles of white wine, a bottle of Chivas Regal and one of Jack Daniel's were quickly ordered by Joseph. Monica and her friends ordered a Margarita, B52, Long Island and some Kahlua.

In the VIP room, there was a pink sofa with two tables. In front of it was a 29-inch television. Monica and her friends, who were still tipsy, began choosing their favourite songs. With jarring voices, they took turns to sing, gulping down even more drinks as they went along.

Half an hour later, I decided to get out of the room, feeling uneasy because if I stayed inside I would be disturbing their privacy. I joined the waitresses who were standing in front of the door. From behind the unveiled curtains, I could see what was going on inside.

Monica had ordered some dancers to further liven up the party. The waitresses usually offered two kinds of packages: the first package was the women to escort them singing, and the second package was the striptease dancers.

Three couples of male and female dancers appeared wearing sexy clothes and they immediately began some very hot moves. Monica and her friends shouted hysterically. The couples then began removing their clothes, with Monica and friends cheering them on.

The three female dancers approached Joseph and JT then sat in their laps. Everyone held their breath as they began pulling off Joseph and JT's clothes. At the same time, the three male dancers moved in closer to Monica, Marcela, Jeny and Shinta.

'Just make them naked!' shouted Shinta.

Even though Joseph and JT tried repeatedly, they could not stop what the female dancers were doing. The dancers' mouths were now very close to Joseph and JT's ears. From their pockets, Joseph and JT took out some hundred thousand rupiah notes. It seemed that as usual the girls wanted to earn tips by seducing the men. As soon as they got their hands on the tips, the dancers began smooching again, even crazier than before.

Monica and the girls experienced the same thing. When one of the male dancers sat on Marcela's lap, she screamed loudly while laughing.

The crazy party with the striptease dancers continued until early in the morning. Eventually, Monica and her friends returned to HG hotel where Monica had booked four rooms.

These wild parties had begun as sporadic events but then became something of a tradition and were organised whenever somebody celebrated a birthday or got a windfall. This could be as often as once a month or even once a week.

What was the real purpose of such a glamorous lifestyle? I wondered.

One time, Shinta invited me to her daughter's wedding party in an elite complex in the Pasar Minggu area. I was fairly surprised because her daughter had not yet finished senior high school, but I was even more startled when I found out that her daughter had been pregnant for about six months. The bridegroom was still too young to become her husband.

A number of Jakarta celebrities and government officers attended the party. Most of the guests were Shinta's best friends, either in her daily social associations or from her business. The wedding party, according to Javanese tradition, continued for two days and two nights. After the party was over, Shinta and her gang—Monica, Jeny, Marcela and Joyce—were seen sitting in a group chatting at the front terrace.

Even though born with a silver spoon and living a glamourous life, Shinta was actually lonely. She could not check her tears when she saw her daughter sit next to her husband in the marriage ceremony. Shinta was getting sadder, especially when she had to sit next to her ex-husband at the marriage ceremony.

Shinta's life was full of problems. The household she founded with her former husband, Dimas, could not be continued any more and for that she was sad. Dimas was famous among the café businessmen in Jakarta. He was the younger sibling of an Indonesian conglomerate owner. After she was divorced from her husband, Shinta lived together with her two children in the Pondok Indah area.

After her divorce from her husband, Shinta began work again as one of the directors at PT ABT, a mining company, and she also found time to run a catering and restaurant business.

She had been divorced for almost nine years. To kill her loneliness, she often spent her time in cafés. It was in such places that she got to know Monica, Joyce, Jeny and Marcela. They were all in the same boat, being lonely divorcees. Such meetings in the café led to a very solid friendship between them all. They lived and breathed each other's problems.

Everyday they tried to spend a certain amount of time together, whether fitness training, having a social gathering, hanging out in some cafés or salons, taking dancing lessons or just to holding crazy parties like the one we had attended.

Shinta admitted that she felt she was living in a pseudo-world. She had no firm ground on which she could plant her feet. The only way to kill her loneliness was to immerse herself in Jakarta's glamorous daily life.

'What else can I do? I don't enjoy being lonely at home,' she said.

Monica was experiencing a similar situation except she was a little happier because she had Joseph, upon whom she could rely. Even though she was only Joseph's mistress, Monica felt that she lost nothing because she was still allowed to do what she liked. She said that her being frustrated due to her broken marriage made her take revenge. Previously, she had been a faithful wife to her husband. Unfortunately, what she got in return was the darkest page of her life— her husband was a philanderer.

Her meeting up with women like Shinta, who had faced similar experiences as her, made her feel as if she had found new ground to justify what they did as a group. A party lifestyle was, for her, not wrong because at least it was a way of life from which she could find some happiness, no matter how vague or blurry it was.

For Monica, it wasn't wrong if there were some people who led a glamorous lifestyle. Such a way of life was not unique to her; everyone she knew also lived it.

Monica and her friends were very fond of holding parties, but they were not drug users.

'We frequently have alcohol, but we aren't drug users. It's not our style,' Monica explained.

If they happened to be seen consuming cocaine, for example, it was because they just wanted to try it.

'We've tried it once or twice, but we aren't regular users,' she admitted.

What simple principles Monica and Shinta had. For them, they simply enjoyed whatever life threw at them at every given moment. They never cared about the negative rumours circulating about their way of life.

'Go to hell with what people say! Everyone has his or her own way of life,' affirmed Monica.

Nor did they care about their status as divorcees. They were easygoing people, but Monica and Shinta were sometimes more worried now that their children were becoming more grown-up.

Once in a while, they had thought about ending their marital status as single divorcees. There were certainly men, who had wanted to marry them, but they hadn't accepted, indeed they liked being free women.

'I really don't know when I can change this way of life,' pondered Shinta.

'Hey, don't forget, tomorrow we're attending a dance class. And in the evening we're going to NZ café,' Marcela reminded Shinta and the others.

It seemed that the dance lessons had become another part of their routine. During our talk, Shinta did not deny that she did such activities just to kill her loneliness. She said that by doing such things she could forget her sadness and suffering.

I hoped that that was working but I was sceptical.

Nude Casinos

In an obscene display of decadence, wealthy businessmen hire the services of nude girls to help sort their piles of coloured chips when betting at the casino tables.

Casinos have long been a feature of Jakarta nightlife and they are widely spread throughout the city. Various types of gambling games are available, such as Pakong, Togel and Singapura. In Central Jakarta, in the Mangga Dua district, there was an elite gambling arena, which became the prime location for men who liked playing with money.

NS could have been in the heart of Las Vegas. It had it all: gambling, nude women and the glamour of nighttime entertainment.

I first heard about this VIP casino and its naked ladies when I made the acquaintance of three girls, Jeny, Dina and Lusy, who were used to accompanying the guests going to gamble at NS.

A friend and I had met the three girls at a television show casting two months before. That brief encounter was followed up with a dinner a week later. It seemed that the three girls were reasonably successful in landing minor roles in local films. Jeny claimed to have been offered some lead roles only that she wasn't really interested because she valued her independence.

'Acting is just for fun. When we used to watch television shows, we thought it would be cool to be the actresses in them,' said Lusy, who had shoulder-length hair.

Some days later the girls invited us to go to their apartment, and of course, we couldn't refuse such an invitation. We then started dropping by now and then just to say hello.

Having met them on several occasions, we were finally getting to know Jeny, Dina, and Lusy's world. They lived in an eighteenth-floor apartment in Hayam Wuruk, not far from SD discotheque, which was open twenty-four hours. The apartment was exclusive, luxurious and conveniently located. Even though the apartment was quite small, it felt luxurious and it was serviced, with similar facilities found in a hotel.

Jeny, Dina and Lusy were, of course, night girls in that their lives were played out during the night—they slept most of the day or relaxed in front of the television—but they were not prostitutes as such.

During my interaction with them, I got lots of information about their profession. Even though men frequently booked them, it was not always connected with buying sex. According to Lusy, she limited herself to accompanying guests to karaoke centres or discotheques.

'At the most, they ask me to sing with them. If we're in discotheques, they ask me to dance or to trip with them,' she said.

Dina and Jeny agreed. They both said that the men whom they usually accompanied mostly needed friends in karaoke bars or discotheques. Although they didn't have sex with the men, they still received lots of money.

'People always think that when we're booked, it must relate to sleeping with them. In fact, it's not like that. Even without the sex, they usually give us big tips. Once I got US$2000 for one night,' said Jeny.

It was from these three girls that I learnt about luxury casinos where big bosses and some elite government officers gambled.

It was ten o'clock at night and I was chatting with Jeny in her room. Dina and Lusy, whose rooms were next to Jeny's, had also joined us. As usual, the topic of our talk was relationships. Local pop songs like Audi's 'Satu Jam Saja' and Paramitha Rusady's 'Cinta' as well as numbers by Jennifer Lopez were playing as we chatted.

Jeny once had a boyfriend from the same hometown, Semarang, but they broke up because her parents didn't agree with her relationship. Meanwhile, Dina talked about her ideal man, AD, who it seemed was admired by all the girls. Meanwhile, Lusy complained about her lover who rarely invited her to go out because he'd already taken a new wife who was more beautiful and younger than she was.

We had been chatting for about an hour when Jeny's new Nokia cell phone rang.

'Sorry, let me just get that,' she said.

We kept quiet as Jeny slowly answered the phone call.

'What's up Pi?' asked Jeny.

There was a short pause.

'OK, Pi. That's fine. What time shall we meet?' she continued. 'Let us get made up first, OK? We'll be there in half an hour.'

Jeny then approached Dina and Lusy and said, 'Papi has just told me that I have to accompany some guests gambling, in the usual place. Could you come with me?'

'Sure, but give us a moment. Let's change our clothes and do our make-up,' said Dina.

'I'll take a shower first. Just stay here. It's fine,' said Jeny to my friend and I, while opening her wardrobe to take out a dark red towel.

Soon after that we heard the sound of water from the shower in her bathroom. We were waiting for Jeny while watching an Armani fashion show on television. Several minutes later, Jeny came out from the bathroom and sat on the bed next to us. She sprinkled some powder over her body and made up her face. Jeny was now wearing a long black gown and high-heeled shoes. As she adjusted her gown, she picked up her cell phone.

'Could you please prepare one car? On behalf of Jeny, Room 505,' she said.

Jeny then looked at herself in the mirror.

'Have you ever been to a casino? Want to join us? This one's great, because it's for the rich. Come on, join us,' she offered.

We accepted her invitation, out of curiosity more than anything else. From behind the door we heard Dina and Lusy's voice.

'Jen, are you ready? We're waiting outside,' they shouted.

We went down two sets of stairs and soon arrived at the front yard, where a car was waiting for us. Jeny, Dina and Lusy were sitting in the middle seats while we were in the back. On the way, Jeny, Dina, and Lusy talked more about the casino.

'Have you ever been there? The place is very convenient. It's great. I bet you'll like it,' said Lusy.

On this particular evening, the three girls had been booked by two Indonesian businessmen. According to the three girls, NS was famous as an elite casino in Jakarta. For the ordinary class, a gambler had to have at least Rp1 million (US$100) to buy chips. For the VIP class, however, a gambler had to prepare a deposit of Rp5 million (US$500).

'We don't join them playing,' Jeny explained. 'We do ask them to buy us some chips but we'll just exchange them later. It's a decent enough amount of money. That doesn't include the tips though, they come later.

'Well, Papi said that tonight's client own many companies. What I've heard is that he's called Mr Liong and that he has cigarette and pulp businesses,' continued Jeny.

Fifteen minutes later we arrived at NS. The traffic in front of NS building was busy, hundreds of cars were parked close by. After entering the building, we got into the lift with three other men.

'The place is on the fourth floor,' said Lusy.

As we stepped out from the lift, we were confronted with a noisy, busy casino. A man appeared and smiled at the three girls.

'Come on in. We've been waiting,' he said.

This, evidently, was Papi. From his back pocket, Papi took out some chips. Jeny gave everybody some chips of varying colours: red, blue, yellow etc.

'With these chips, we can enter the casino. If you want to try your luck, you can use them to play,' she said.

We separated from Jeny at the entrance door. After Jeny, Dina and Lusy disappeared among the crowds of gamblers, we decided to have a look around. For twenty minutes we walked around the gambling arena, looking at the people trying their luck on the tables. In the middle of the room, we saw Jeny, Dina and Lusy accompanying their three men, who were gambling at one of the casino tables. Jeny was accompanying a fairly fat man wearing glasses, while Dina and Lusy were accompanying two other men who were of medium build and smartly dressed. Two men sat on the other two chairs, and were also accompanied by two beautiful girls.

An intense game was underway. Hoarse, disappointed voices were heard from some of the men. Jeny's man thrust ten chips forward. Smiling, he whispered intimately to Jeny. The other four men were doing the same thing. A sense of victory was apparent on the face of the man accompanied by Jeny.

We were right. Jeny's man was to be the lucky one. A broad smile adorned his red cheeks, as his hands scooped up the coins. A moment later, he hugged Jeny tightly and kissed her left cheek repeatedly.

Treated in such a way, Jeny could just writhe, and if she felt uncomfortable, she didn't show it. Jeny, Dina and Lusy accepted what the men did in an indulgent way, while laughing flirtatiously.

The view at the other casino tables was similar. There were tens of casino tables full of women and men who were trying their luck.

All of a sudden, we were startled by the presence of a well-built man.

'Hey, what are you doing here?' said the man.

'Hey, Bert. It's you! And what are you doing here?' we asked him.

The stocky guy was Robert, a security guard who often guarded wealthy businessmen and the children of important government officers.

'As usual, I'm guarding the boss,' he replied.

In fact, what Robert meant by the boss was an Indonesian businessman who had many companies and had a close relationship with a local Chinese businessman. Besides being fond of gambling at the casino, Robert's boss, named HR, frequently hung out at some of the elite cafés in Jakarta.

'Don't just stand there doing nothing, follow me. I'll show you something amazing,' said Robert.

We just nodded, as Robert then took us to another entrance door not far from the standard-class casino tables. Soon after we passed through the doorway, we saw some rooms that were closely guarded. It appeared there were at least ten VIP casino rooms at NS and they reminded us of the karaoke room at the BK discotheque in Surdiman area.

'My boss is playing in that room,' said Robert, pointing to a room guarded by two men. The room was named after a state in America.

'Let's just stay here. Boss usually plays until early in the morning,' explained Robert while sitting on a sofa.

According to Robert, his boss was gambling with four rich businessmen. We asked who they were.

'I'm not sure. One of them has a mineral water plant,' he said.

We chatted with Robert for about thirty minutes as he waited faithfully in front of the door.

'What's so exciting then? You said you'd show us something,' I gently reminded him.

'You want to see it? OK. But please be quiet,' said Robert.

He then slowly opened the door. Behind the door was a black curtain. Robert inched the curtain apart. And ... my goodness! We could clearly see a round table around which five men were sitting and playing cards. Robert's boss, who was sitting quietly, was wearing a polo shirt and a pair of glasses.

What made us open our eyes wide were the three girls who stood around the table. The girls were wearing nothing. They were completely naked! Their postures were very sensual. Two of them had smooth, beautiful skin and 32B-figures. One of the girls, who had shoulder-length curly hair, was standing on the left of the table, had an incredible 32D-figure, which was very eye catching!

'The girl with the big breasts is Mona. She's twenty-one years old, from Manado,' whispered Robert.

Mona reminded us of the face of an Indonesian sex-bomb from the 1990s called SM. Her lips were red and her eyes were ever so tempting.

Like Guest Relation Officers (GROs) who accompanied guests for dinner or drinks in some cafés, Mona and the other girls were on hand to serve the bosses with whatever they needed, whether it be pouring some drinks or distributing the cards.

From behind the door veiled with the black curtain, our hearts were beating faster as we watched the girls' behaviour. We were astonished when we saw what the five men were doing to the three naked girls. When one of the men won the game, he immediately asked one of the girls to collect and sort the pile of chips. There were hundreds of chips. The value of some of the chip was as high as Rp1 million (US$100)—the mind boggles! After collecting his winnings and roaring with laughter, the winner hugged the girl intimately. Well, actually, his hands rubbed the girl's nude body.

'We won again, honey,' said one man who was sitting with his back to us while hugging the girl's waist. The girl didn't balk at all at what the man was doing.

What the three girls were doing reminded us of what Jeny, Dina and Lusy did when they accompanied their men in the standard-class casino. We wondered if Jeny and her friends also accompanied the men in the same way, i.e. in the nude.

'OK, that's enough. If they knew what I was doing, I'd be fired,' said Robert, reminding us how lucky we were to be witnessing this.

That door to another world was closed again. We found ourselves back outside on the sofa waiting once again. From our discussion with Robert, we knew that the three girls were booked through a famous procurer in Jakarta.

'My boss ordered them. I picked them up from their boarding house in Batu Ceper,' said Robert.

Robert claimed that the nude girls had been a regular feature in the VIP rooms for some time. Apparently, each girl was paid Rp3 million (US$300). But such an amount of money was nothing compared to the tips they pocketed.

After talking to Robert for several hours we decided to check out the main casino as it was already approaching four in the morning. Robert ordered one of his subordinates, John, to accompany us around the casino. We wandered over to the standard-class tables and observed what was happening. It seemed that NS also provided slot machines, like Mickey Mouse, Happy Royal and keno.

We witnessed some interesting things. One of the players was in the process of pawning his possessions. This was nothing new at NS casino

'The latest Nokia cell phone can be pawned for Rp500,000 (US$50) to Rp1 million (US$100),' explained John. 'There are even some luxury cars like Mercs and BMWs that are pawned here at a very low price. Lots of people here are gambling while waiting for more pawned items to arrive.'

John suggested that if we had cash, we'd better hang around the casino. It seemed that there were many bargains to be had by the early morning!

At around five thirty in the morning, we decided to go back to see Robert. It seemed that the card game in the VIP room was over. From the room came the sound of loud music.

'My boss won many times. He got more than Rp700 million [US$700],' said Robert when we approached him. 'Now, they're having a party.'

What kind of party? we wondered. Thanks to Robert, we peeped through the door once more, which was still veiled with a black curtain. The three naked girls were dancing around the casino table. Perhaps they were professional dancers, we thought.

The atmosphere in the VIP casino room had changed. It was now filled with laughter and the sound of clinking glasses. The early-morning party was hotting up. Hundred-thousand- and fifty-thousand-denomination notes were strewn across the floor. The three girls were picking up the scattered money from the floor in a playful and erotic manner.

The three girls were wet with beads of their sweat covering their bodies. The five bosses who had betted billions of rupiah at the casino table were totally captivated. They were heard laughing boastfully whenever they scattered the money on the floor.

Robert closed the door very slowly. We asked him where he would take his boss after this.

'We'll be going home directly,' he replied. 'Even though my boss has hired the girls, he's never invited them to sleep with him. When the gambling is over, they are just asked to go home. That's it.'

We said goodbye and left the place. On the way to the lift, we saw tens of people queuing in front of the cage, where they could exchange their chips for cash. We arrived on the ground floor at almost seven in the morning. Through our cell phones we said goodbye to Jeny and her friends.

The sun appeared shyly, its rays sparkled over the city. Our minds were still getting to grips with the thought of three naked girls dancing around card table for the wealthy businessmen. What was becoming of Jakarta?

We could only shake our heads.

Foreign Imports

No less financially desperate than their Indonesian counterparts, buxom, blue-eyed, (bleach) blondes from Uzbekistan, Russia and even Mexico are now regular features on the Jakarta sex circuit. Few in number, they charge high prices and hope to save enough to return home with a profit.

The story began when I met thirty-four-year-old businessman, Nicolas, who had been running an entertainment and advertising business for about eight years, which was steadily becoming more successful and profitable. Every month Nicolas held a number of entertainment events in various clubs, cafés and discotheques. Nicolas not only ran his business in Jakarta but also in other large Indonesian cities including Surabaya, Bandung and Medan.

Actually, Nicolas and I had known each other for quite some time. This was because as an entertainment mogul, Nicolas was almost inseparable from the clubbing world. Not only was he well known in any number of fashionable entertainment venues in Jakarta, he was also a trendsetter in the world of night entertainment. The events that he held were always innovative and full of new ideas.

'As a man from the world of entertainment, I have to know the latest trends. Going to cafés or discotheques is part of my self-socialization. Besides, I'm still single,' Nicolas said jokingly.

Talking to Nicolas helped me to gain a little more inside knowledge of the Jakarta nightlife and he was kind enough to invite me to attend several functions including an event held in a popular entertainment place called SS, in the city centre. The idea behind the event at SS was very simple. Besides inviting a number of beautiful models for a fashion show, he also invited three famous DJs. However, to make the event more exciting, Nicolas employed six striptease dancers who would perform for the public. Seldom were striptease dancers paraded in front of the public—usually they danced in private rooms; if not in karaoke centres, in a hotel room or in a private house. This event proved very successful and attracted around 600 guests.

On another occasion, Nicolas invited me to join him in a VIP karaoke room, also at SS. By coincidence, Nicolas had a little surprise in store because his close friend had just arrived from Batam. Besides, he also wanted to throw a small party to celebrate his recent business success. During the past three months he had organised at least twelve events in different entertainment venues and most of the events had made him big profits.

'Well, let's say it's just a small celebration. Sharing happiness with friends isn't a crime, is it?' he said, while smiling.

I was due to meet Nicolas at the VIP room at ten o'clock. Luckily, I had been to SS before, so I found it easily. Having spoken to Nicolas on the phone earlier, I knew he would be waiting with two of his friends. After parking my car on the fourth level of the carpark, I went straight up to the karaoke joint.

On the way, I passed a Japanese restaurant full of diners. Glancing in to the restaurant it struck me as odd that there were lots of beautiful girls wearing sexy clothes sitting around in groups. Some were busy chatting while others just sat watching the guests coming into the restaurant.

At the entrance to the karaoke centre, two female receptionists bade me enter. Inside was another small restaurant, where karaoke guests could relax for a meals and drinks. A lift connected the restaurant to the basement where the VIP karaoke rooms were located.

Stepping out of the lift I was confronted by an assemblage of beautiful girls. They were what people called singers, madames or according to the term used at SS called GROs (Guest Relations Officers). Some of them were joking and laughing together, others watched the television. Newly arriving guests took the time to smile at the girls because they expected to be placing an order for a date in a karaoke room.

The male guests could not stand there admiring the view all day though—a waitress would steer them into whichever room that had booked. As was the case with me.

'Hey, you're thirty minutes late. You're lucky, the party hasn't started yet,' said Nicolas when I entered the room.

The VIP room was fairly dim. In the middle of the room was a light brown sofa and a wooden table. In front of it were four 29-inch televisions. The television sets were neatly positioned in a long cupboard. Behind the TV console was a dining table and a very exclusive bedroom like you would expect to find in a smart hotel. A luxury bathroom was attached. That's rather bizarre, I thought. The bathroom was located next to the karaoke room so you would have to walk through it to reach the bedroom.

On the wall next to the TV console were two long doors. At a glance, the two doors looked like they belonged to a built-in wardrobe but, my goodness, as soon as the doors were open, we were presented with a view, through glass windows, of the bathroom. While sitting on the sofa singing karaoke, guests could see everything going on in the bathroom.

Judging from the audio-visual equipment, it was clear that SS was more progressive than other karaoke centers. Not only could the four TVs be used to display karaoke songs but they could also be used as karaoke menus to choose songs, as food menus to order meals and as GRO menus to order girls! This last menu listed the GRO's names, height, weight and even their bust size!

Nicolas and his two friends were sitting on the sofa. Nicolas introduced the two guys as Arman and Johan. Both were Nicolas's close friends who had been in Jakarta for two days; they were from Batam, where they ran a restaurant business.

'In Batam, the kings are Arman and Johan. If you want to know the night world in Batam, these two guys are the experts,' said Nicolas while looking at his friends.

Praised in such a fashion, the two guys, who were dressed casually, were smiling bashfully.

On the table was a bottle of Jack Daniel's, Coca-Cola and ice, several plates of snacks and two big bowls of fresh fruit. It seemed that Nicolas and his two friends had already sung at least eight numbers. Therefore, by the time I arrived, Nicolas was ready to take the party to the next level.

'Hey, it's cold in here if there's no women. How about we order two or three girls to warm up the party?' said Nicolas.

Nicolas's friends and I nodded in agreement but before Nicolas could summon the waitress who was on duty, Johan made a request. According to Johan, he was bored with local escort girls. He said that in Batam he could easily get local girls and shouldn't we go for something a little different?

'So, you want imported girls? Just be cool my friend. Everything can be arranged. You know, they offer a very complete service here,' said Nicolas confidently.

Nicolas then got up and left the room for several minutes. I wasn't surprised because as an entertainment tycoon, Nicolas certainly knew the people at SS well—from the wait staff and managers, to the owner. At least once a month, Nicolas would hold an event of his own at SS.

No more than ten minutes later, Nicolas came back to his seat. He was smiling and looked pleased with himself. He picked up a glass of Jack Daniel's with ice, inviting us to drink together.

While waiting for our order to be delivered, we talked some more while watching the television, which was relaying the hit songs we requested. Because I'm not really good at singing, I just tried the one song.

To my relief, some minutes later our order was delivered. It was already eleven o'clock when two sexy women appeared at the door. They immediately joined us at the sofa and introduced themselves.

The first girl was of medium height and had long, straight blond hair and round eyes. She had an oval face and thin lips, which she painted with red lipstick. She introduced herself as Susan. Meanwhile, the second girl was called Caroline. She had curly, shoulder-length brown hair. Caroline was not as tall as Susan, but she was just as hot. The V-shaped dress that Caroline was wearing fit the contours of her body well.

From the outset we spoke to the girls in English and their accents sounded a bit strange. Naturally curious, I paid close attention to Susan and Caroline's mannerisms, from the way they spoke to their appearance. I tried to guess where they were from.

The party was livening up. I got more intimate with the girls as we toasted together, drinking three or four glasses in the space of about ten minutes. The courtesy session was finally over. Susan and Caroline seemed to understand what was expected of them. The music was changed; Mariah Carey's 'My All' was replaced by garage music. On the TV screen, erotic dancing flashed before us.

Susan and Caroline then got up from the sofa and walked over to the bathroom. While waiting for them I was enjoying the erotic dance on the TV. The beautiful girls who had perfect bodies began to remove their clothes. It was when all of the girls on the TV were naked that Susan and Caroline came out from the bathroom.

I'd guessed correctly that they had wanted to change their clothes. Susan now wore tight black clothes, while Caroline was wearing tight blue hot pants and a tank top, which revealed a piercing on her navel. Meanwhile, on Susan's back was a tattoo depicting a black dragon.

They began dancing exotically in front of us so, without needing too much encouragement, I shifted my gaze from the TV screen to look at the live show featuring Susan and Caroline.

The two girls, who finally revealed they came from Uzbekistan, began to move their bodies in an erotic fashion. Their moves were similar to the local striptease dancers performing elsewhere in Jakarta but, because they were foreigners, what I saw reminded me more of pubs or discotheques in Amsterdam, Holland, or in Las Vegas.

Susan and Caroline danced with abandon. Their tight clothes no longer concealed their bodies, they were naked. The cold air from the air-conditioner wasn't really having any effect—such was the sexual heat in the air.

Slowly they danced closer to each other. Their naked bodies were like butterflies flittering from one flower to the next. Susan and Caroline were not only dancing but also starting to caress and pet us, and even crouch before us like a tiger ready to pounce on its prey.

Whenever their prey, one of us, was aching with desire the girls only prolonged the seduction until we could take it no longer and took from our pockets wads of hundred-thousand-denomination notes.

It seemed that their tricks were exactly the same as those of the local girls. All the girls at SS were singers, performed striptease dancing, gave the NHS (no hand service) and provided a full service if so requested.

Usually, there were two ways of choosing the girls. First, the guests could select the girls from the Japanese restaurant. It seemed that the girls hanging around in groups in the restaurant were singers, escort girls and dancers. More often, though, the guests directly chose the girls in the karaoke rooms. They ordered the dancers through the on-duty waitresses or directly through the mammy, then would choose their favourites from at least four to six girls. Such a process applied to local and foreign dancers alike. What also frequently happened was that the girls did a kind of parade, walking around the discotheque and restaurant.

'If we're members here, it's easier. We don't need to bother ourselves choosing the girls. Because members usually get the best,' explained Nicolas.

After Susan and Caroline had warmed up the room with their erotic dancing, they progressed to offering NHS. It was during this phase that they began receiving big tips from the other guys. With their flattery, their mouths could easily spell out a certain number. With just one delicate touch to the immobile guest, they could get Rp200,000 to Rp300,000 (US$20 to US$30).

Usually, after they got their opening tips, they would continue seducing the guests until they reached a stage where they could negotiate for a full service. The full service was the most important opportunity for the dancers to earn as much money as possible.

In order to get the full service in the private karaoke room with an Indonesian girl, a guest would be expected to give the girl tips of between Rp300,000 to Rp500,000 (US$30 to US$50). The exact amount depended on the agreement reached between both parties.

Compare this with the prices charged for the imported girls. Just to book a striptease dance service, a dancer had to be paid at least Rp3 million (US$300). This didn't include the cost for the room, which could be reserved for at least three hours. The cost per hour was Rp100,000 (US$10) for a standard room and Rp200,000 (US$20) for a VIP room. The Royal Suite cost between Rp300,000 and Rp400,000 (US$30 and US$40) an hour. The Royal Suite was as plush as a suite in a five-star hotel.

Not all guests at SS karaoke directly satisfied their lust on the spot. Some of them chose to book the imported girls after their working hours. But the tariff was much higher; it could be twice as much as the normal tariff. If a guest wanted to take them out from SS for a one-night stand, he had to pay at least Rp5 to 6 million (US$500 to 600).

Whereas a guest would have to pay tips of around Rp300,000

to 500,000 (US$30 to 50) in order to get the full service from local Indonesian dancers, for the imported striptease dancers a guest had to spend at least Rp500,000 or Rp1 million (US$50 to US$100). A lot more money that may be but it was nothing for rich men who liked spending their cash at SS.

This was obvious from Nicolas and his friends' behaviour. After Susan and Caroline mesmerised them with NHS tricks, the men spent around Rp400,000 to Rp500,000 (US$40 to US$50). Then, after Susan whispered her magic words in Nicolas' ear, he was like a water buffalo being led by the nose. The same thing happened with Arman.

Finally only Johan and I were left sitting on the sofa, waiting for Nicolas and Arman to satisfy their lustful desires. In order to kill the time in the room, we were watching the striptease dancing relayed on the TV in front of us. I lost count of how many glasses of Jack Daniel's we downed in less than fifteen minutes.

Susan and Nicolas finally appeared from the bedroom; soon after, Arman and Caroline came out from the bathroom. The two men smiled contentedly at us. Susan and Caroline were still naked; from the look in their eyes, it might well be our turn now!

Susan and Caroline slowly approached us like models strutting their stuff on the catwalk. Nicolas and Arman were now laughing uproariously. Damn! I could only get the leftovers, I thought. Before I had a chance to react, Caroline suddenly sat on my lap. My earlier prophecy seemed to be right: Susan was leading Johan to the bathroom, while Caroline took my hand, guiding me to the bedroom.

Acknowledgements

First of all, I would like to thank Heriyadi H. Sobiran, the 'elder' at *Popular* magazine, who not only supported me wholeheartedly but also graciously granted me permission to reproduce a number of articles that previously appeared in the magazine under the column 'Entertainment for Men'.

Thanks are also due to Mujimanto Asmotaruno, the 'chief' at *Male Emporium (ME)* magazine, who demonstated the skills required to master a style of writing that is both interesting and stimulating to read, and who was resposible for knocking many of my articles into shape during his time at *Popular*.

I am also indebted to Mas Basbardono, who taught me what beautiful prose is supposed to look like while we were colleagues at *Berita Yudha* and *Prospek*. It seemed that every article I wrote became more beautiful after being edited by him. Congratulations, Mas Bas, on your book *Selingkuh*.

Thank you Mas Dadi Darmadi, my 'brother', who motivated me and showed me a way of life at university. I am still eargerly awaiting the publication of your book!

Finally, I would like to thank Ita Sembiring, who was instrumental in binging to fruition the original Indonesian-language edition of this book; Dr Dede Oetomo for his updated Foreword for this English-language edition; Mas Julius of Galang Press; Rizal Mantovani, who is always up for a scholarly discussion; and the young people of Menteng who shared their stories with me and who became good friends. Dodi, Miko, Yudi, Lisa, Didit, Mas Eko, Susi, Erwin, Lita, Melly, April, Trie, Wisnu, Mori, Satria, Ucok, Jimmy, Dolop etc ... you guys rock!